All Things in Christ
Methodist Prayer Handbook 2007/08

CW00386541

LAST SUMMER I moved to a house with a mature garden. A well-established planting scheme needs to be treated with respect, but weeding and pruning will refresh and bring new life.

This year I have tried to keep what is best about the Prayer Handbook, while updating and reinvigorating it with the help of your comments, the results of a reader questionnaire we carried out last year and, as ever, the wisdom and guidance of the Prayer Handbook Committee. I have tried to include prayers from as many as possible of our much-loved established authors, while providing space for many contributions from keen new ones.

You will notice that, as well as a fresh design, we have brought the lectionary into the middle of the book.

sectic

have it to hand each day. Do email me at editorial@quantrillmedia.com and let me know what you think.

I have also commissioned new maps, including a world map in full colour. It makes sense, particularly with this year's theme of 'All Things in Christ' to view the world as a whole. Despite the familiar politial borders displayed on the map, God holds all our precious earth in his hands. He has no need for political, social, racial and geographical boundaries.

The wind blows where it pleases (John 3.8) and the waters of the oceans are one water. Let us take care of them and of our brothers and sisters who live on other shores.

Primavera Quantrill

How to use this book

The Prayer Handbook is arranged as a monthly cycle, starting with Day 1 of the month on page 8. You can use the book as a focus for your daily prayer and start the cycle again at the beginning of each month, or just dip in at random. You could add your own notes in the margins to remind you of things you would like to pray for on particular days. If you are leading a group or praying on your own you might find it helpful to select just a few of the prayers for the day. You might also want to add prayers for the people listed at the side of the page. There are general prayers at the beginning (pages 2-7) which you can pick and choose according to your needs – or you can just dip in. In the centre of the Handbook (pages 37-44) there is a pull-out lectionary which suggests readings and psalms for each day of the year. Either side of this you will find a beautifully illustrated prayer by St Francis, with short verses arranged by the days of the week – ideal for more contemplative prayer, or if you don't have much time. However you use this resource you know you are joining withour Methodist brothers and sisters all around Britain and the world.

Praise for God the creator

The stars in the heavens define your
    awesome greatness;
the sun your boundless energy;
mountains and seas your
    powerful presence.
Who am I before such a God as this?
What hope of being noticed?
What matter my needs or concerns?
Or those of my neighbour?

Yet this same God
invites me to call him 'Abba', 'Father';
to be a daughter, a son
and invites my neighbour to do the same;
invites me to share my pilgrimage
through life in his company;
and my neighbour to do the same.

Lord, help me to remember your
presence
day after day, hour after hour,
minute after minute.
In all that I say and do and experience
make me open and receptive
to being blessed by you
through my neighbour.
And through me
may that same neighbour be encircled
and enriched by your blessing.

Ward Jones, Bristol District Chair

The tree of life (Gen.2.9 and Rev. 22.2)
Christ is the tree
helping us climb towards God.
Our life with Christ
is climbing the tree
like adventurous children.

Sometimes it's hard
to find a foothold in Jesus Christ.
Dogmatic knots and
ring upon ring of tradition
can make complex a simple trust,
the next move in Christ's branches.

Christ is the apple tree
laden with fruit, always green;
is the gnarled oak,
ancient yet sturdy;
is enveloped in vines,
the rain-drenched tree in a
    tropical forest.

We are the fruit
of 12 different kinds,
held together in Christ's
tree of life.

Francesca Rhys,
Probationer Minister, Leeds

Lord our God, almighty and infinite creator of forests and
mountains, rivers and seas, maker of the sky and planets of
the universe, we believe in you and we want to praise and
glorify your holy name. But our human faith is often so small,
so puny and self-centred, so confined to our own narrow
vision and limited understanding. Increase our faith in you,
enlarge our vision of your kingdom, expand our knowledge
and experience of your Spirit and your ways, until we are fully
part of your great purpose for the salvation of the world,
through Jesus Christ our Lord. Amen.

Ivan McElhinney, former President, Methodist Church in Ireland

Praise for Christ our Saviour

All things in Christ

all
loving God
you are my all
you are all I am
and all I need
and all I can ever be

all things
come from you
all things
belong to you
all things
return to you

all things in
me and my life
my hopes and fears
my sickness and health
my work, my education, my leisure
all things in
the world and creation
in poverty and riches
in struggles for justice and equality
all things in
earth and heaven
all things in
time and space and eternity
all things are in Christ
all things in Christ

Stephen Poxon,
North Lancashire District Chair

Intercession
(Based on Hymns & Psalms 460)
Inviting God,
who lays the fine table of the earth,
and lying upon the cross
bids all humankind
come near, receive and share.

We pray for souls who
can find no peace,
oppressed
by sin and self and structures,
poor and visionless in body and spirit;
flinching from your freeing love

that your conspiring grace
will be received and known,
resistance replaced with consent,
your word of life lived
and the feast that is Christ be fully
found
in all your creation. Amen.

Martyn Atkins, President of the British
Methodist Conference 2007-8

Thank you, God, for the cross.
We remember that our Saviour was wounded by us and for us
and suffers with us. Give relief today to all who suffer.
Thank you, God, for the resurrection.
We rejoice that our Lord was raised and that life reigns over death. Give hope today
to all who are bereaved.
Thank you, God, for the promised return of Christ.
We reaffirm that Jesus our King calls us to be history-makers. Revive your Church
today with passion and purpose in the doing of your will in your world.
O God our Saviour, Lord and King, we readily profess this day that Christ has died,
Christ is risen and Christ will come again, and in the strong name of Christ we offer
our prayers. Amen.

Ken Todd, Down District Superintendent

Discernment and vocation

Loving God, who sent your Son into the world to die for me, I praise you.
Loving God, who sent your Son into the world to die for all, may the entire world give you praise.
Jesus, my Saviour, may I never forget that I am where I am by your saving grace so freely given to me.
Jesus, Saviour of the world, may more and more people open their hearts to receive your grace so freely given for them.
Spirit of the living God, fill my life to overflowing, that I may not falter on my Christian journey and that I may always show love to those round about me.
Spirit of the living God, move within the hearts of all those who live without you, that they may be directed to walk the right path and that they too may be filled with love. Amen.

Keith Rothery, National Advocate,
Leaders of Worship and Preachers' Trust

Father, we thank you for the awesome privilege of worshipping you and praising you – to go beyond the veil and enter into your holy presence.
You are the omniscient, omnipresent, one creator of the universe.
How wondrous and beautiful you are in your splendour, how gracious and true.
Father, you have created us in your image, and you are love itself.
Make us worthy recipients of that perfect love – enable us to show and share it, drawing others to yourself. Amen.

Maureen Thomson, Appleton Roebuck

Encouraging, enabling and
    equipping God,
at the dawning of a new day,
open our eyes afresh
to the wonders and miracles
that surround us.

Encourage us, enable us and equip us
for the challenges that we
    will face today,
for the injustices that we shall see
and for the poverty we
    shall encounter.

Encourage us, enable us and equip us
to be proactive and positive,
to release your energy of love
into the world,
and to seek peace wherever we tread,
in your name.

Encouraging, enabling and
    equipping God,
encircle us with your strength
and with your love
this day and for evermore. Amen.

Adam Dyjasek, Methodist Church
Committee for Gender Justice

In-dwelling God,
you create all that is,
bring us to discern
your hand and mind
in all your works,
and so serve you
with joy and thankfulness.

Terry Miller, Chaplain for the Environment
and Sustainable Development,
Lincolnshire Chaplaincy Services

Personal wholeness and the integrity of creation

Gracious God,
we thank you that your desire for us
    is life in full fruitfulness.
We thank you for filling our lives
    with good things:
for hibiscus and breadfruit,
    coral and conch,
for mangroves and whale sharks,
    iguanas and red snapper,
for precious people and the power of love.
We are sorry that we carelessly pollute
the beauty of earth and ocean,
reef and swamp, body and soul.
We pray for wisdom to choose the way
    that leads to abundant life.
We pray for strength to resist and remove
    all that harms or degrades life.
We pray for love, in Christ,
    to be committed
to the well-being of all life. Amen.

Janet Corlett, Mission Partner,
Bay Islands, Honduras

O Lord, how gracious and majestic
you are!
As we look at creation we see the power
at your disposal.
As we read the Holy Scriptures, hope
is instilled in us as we try to grasp your
desire to be intimate with us.
As we see the smiling face and extended
hand of help, we see your love for all.
Yet we also see how vulnerable you are.
We see how hurt you are when we hurt
your creation – the world and us in it.
How your hands and side bleed as we
behave unlovingly to your universe
and all in it.
Continue to have mercy upon us.
May your long-suffering and infinite
patience win us over to your heart and
way and unite us around the gospel
feast. Amen.

Edwin Myers, South African Minister
currently working in East Anglia

Prayer for wholeness
Loving God,
when we are overwhelmed by pain
in body, mind or spirit,
help us to open our eyes to see you.

When the ground beneath us is uncertain
and we are confused and fearful,
help us to reach out and grasp your
outstretched hand.

When we are oppressed by guilt,
help us to grasp the good news
of your forgiveness,
to know that all mistakes
and regrets from our past
are transformed in the purity of your love.

In our brokenness, lift us up;
in our despair, give us hope;
in our loneliness,
remind us of your unfailing presence.

Then, through faith and in newness of life,
may we know each day,
that we are healed by your grace,
held in your love,
encouraged by your Spirit
and given strength to face the journey
ahead. Amen.

Maureen Edwards, former editor of the
Methodist Prayer Handbook

Release Me
To be true
to my inner self,
to be all
that you might long to be in me;

Lord, this is my desire.

Release me, Lord,
to be
the me

not of my dreams,

but of yours.

© Pat Marsh
from 'Silent Strength' published by Inspire

The kinship of all humanity

Generous and welcoming God, who
invites everyone to the greatest
    feast of all,
we pray for people who are rejected
and excluded from the best this world
has to offer because others do not
appreciate them.
May they know that you love and value
them and may they see that reflected
in the love, support and care shown by
your followers to our neighbours.

Encouraging and restoring God, who
offers good news to the poor
    and suffering,
we pray for those who are homeless,
hungry, lonely, ill and bereaved;
may they experience your comfort
and healing and recognize you in the
love, support and care shown by your
followers to our neighbours.

Loving and forgiving God, who
constantly seeks reconciliation
    with every person,
we pray for people whose lives appear
to be full but are too often empty;
may they see glimpses of you in even the
most unexpected places and recognize
you in the love, support and care shown
by your followers to our neighbours.

Eternal and inspiring God, who has been
revealed to people throughout the ages,
we pray that each one of us might
embrace all that you offer to us;
may we too respond to your call
now and live for you, and for all our
neighbours, showing the love, support
and care which reflects your love for all.
Amen.

*Ruby Beech, Vice-President
of the British Methodist Conference 2007-8*

You made each and every one of us, Lord.
Whatever our colour, shape or age,
regardless of our customs,
languages and beliefs,
nothing can separate us from our kinship
with you and with one another.
Barriers, distance, even death
cannot destroy the bond that unites us,
for a part of you lives within us,
eternally linking mind to mind,
soul to soul and heart to heart.
Help us to recognize you in each other,
and to remember our connection
with all people,
even those we find hard
to understand and love.
For we belong together as a family,
each a part of the whole,
with you, our Creator, Saviour
    and Comforter
holding us close to your heart, evermore.
Amen.

*Marilyn Dore, Local Preacher,
Aylesbury Vale Circuit*

God of the villages and God of the cities,
we thank you that you created
    all people equal,
we thank you that you love and value us
all, wherever we were born.
Forgive us when we forget that all people
are made in your image;
forgive us when we see another shocking
statistic from a far-off country and are
unmoved; when we cannot face the needs
of this broken world.
When we feel helpless to challenge the
injustices of this world, give us strength;
help us not to tire of doing good.
Show us how, even through small actions,
we can lead lives that give glory to you,
helping our neighbours in your world.
Amen.

Isabelle Carboni, MRDF

Worship and praise

Give us words to sing your praises,
    Give us music to inspire;
Harmonies and tunes and phrases,
    Words for pulpit, pew and choir.
Words of faith and revelation,
    Words to sing and words to say;
Words of prayer and proclamation:
    Word Incarnate, here today.

Give us hearts that feel contrition
    For the scope of human sin;
Anguish at the earth's condition,
    Sorry for the wrong within.
Through the greed which knows no limit,
    Through suspicion, fear and strife,
Speak to us, rebuking Spirit,
    Guide us to a fairer life.

Give us hands to reach to others
    As we travel on life's ways,
Pilgrim sisters, pilgrim brothers,
    Sharing bright and darker days;
Hands of peace and affirmation,
    Hands for service, glad and free,
Raised in praise and consecration:
    God Eternal, Trinity.

Audrey Stanley
Metre: 8787D
Tune: Hyfrydol, Bethany or Pilgrim Brothers
Published with other winning entries to the
Tercentenary Hymn challenge by The New Room

All things in Christ seem darker now.
The reflection from his glorious light
reveals the emptiness of much we grasp
and shows the way that we should walk.

All things in Christ are brighter now.
His mighty love illumines all;
his presence transforms the darkest hour
as he walks with us, our Saviour and Lord.

All things in Christ are hopeful now.
His grace sets free what once was bound;
with joy unleashed we face each day
in him the price of peace is paid.

All things in Christ are eternal now.
Our God made man has called us home;
the door with which we locked him out,
in Christ alone is opened wide.

All things in Christ are challenged now.
His living presence heals our blindness;
at last we see his broken world
to which he sends us to prove his love.
Amen.

David Clowes, Minister, Wigan Circuit
This prayer will appear in David's book '500 more prayers
for Special Occasions' to be published by Kingsway in 2008.

Our loving, heavenly Father,
we thank you for this time in which we are able to pause in your presence and listen.
We thank you for those occasions when you open our eyes in the quietness and
remind us of moments in our lives when you have been very close to us.
You remind us of people we have met who have guided and helped us along life's way.
We remember those who, realized you were calling us to carry out some work for you
and guided us in the direction you required.
We thank you for those who meet us and inform us that they committed their lives to
you because of some word we uttered in your name. Amen.

John Lawley, Much Wenlock

Day 1

Praying with all creation

Gracious God, with each returning day may we face our concerns and duties with goodness and grace. Let us be cheerful in our undertakings, faithful in business and able to reach the day's end with contentment and honour; through Christ our Lord. Amen.

Robert Louis Stevenson, 1850-94

Almighty God, the splendour and beauty of your creation is all around us but we often fail to see it. Help us to make time in our busy lives to enjoy the work of your hands – flowers in resplendent colours, clear blue skies, clouds heavy with rain, gently swaying trees, the song of a robin, the babbling of a brook, sunrise and sunset. There is just so much, if only we open our eyes and see. Thank you for giving them to us so freely. May we appreciate and be always mindful of your wonderful creation. In Jesus' name we pray. Amen.

Sarah Jason, Mission Partner in training,
Selly Oak Centre for Mission Studies

Prayer of thanks
God of love, Mother, Father and God of many faces,
    thank you for:
the vividness of nature's colours,
the busy activities of the ants,
birdsong,
the unconditional love of our pets,
the smile of an acquaintance as they pass us in the street.
your words spoken directly to us by strangers –
    your angels in disguise –
your presence that is forever with us in the midst of our daily lives wherever we are. Amen.

Sue Jansen, Mission Partner in Argentina

All in Jesus.
All of heaven and all of earth.
Jesus in the living water,
Jesus in the fiery mountain,
Jesus in the breath of Spirit.
Jesus, fill us with living water,
your blazing fire, the breath of your Spirit.
Empower us to bring the life of heaven here on earth. Amen.

Inspired by John 4
Josette Crane, Local Preacher, Keynsham, Bath

Top 3 images Diane Coleman
Bottom image © PureStockX

Prayer for the Connexion
From heights of Herma Ness and Buchan Head,
by Dungeness Point, on Torquay Bay sand,
in East Anglia fen, on Cardigan Bay shore,
on Snaefell summit and Langdale Pikes' top,
together may we celebrate the grandeur of God.
Through tongues Welsh, Doric, Cockney, Geordie or Scouse,
in Ramsey harbour, Felixstowe container port,
to tourists in St Helier, walkers on the Pennine Way,
London commuters, surfers in Newquay,
together may we communicate the Word of God.
Near Dunblane Cathedral, in cosmopolitan Birmingham,
in Honiton town, on campus at Lampeter,
on Salisbury Plain manoeuvres, in Malta, on Gibraltar Rock,
whoever we are, wherever we are
together, may we witness to the Love of God.

Jenny Easson, Local Preacher, Dundee

Loving God, hear our prayers
for all members of the Connexional Team;
for the Methodist Council, the Strategy and Resources
Committee and the Connexional Leadership Team;
for volunteers, working group and committee members;
and for the work done by so many people on behalf
of the Church.
We pray for those who face changes;
grant courage and peace in the midst of uncertainty.
We pray for those who must make difficult decisions;
grant vision and sensitivity to all who bear great responsibility.
We pray that we will continue to listen to one another
with love, patience and care,
that the world might know more of Christ's love
through all our labours. Amen.

Michaela Youngson, Secretary for Pastoral Care and Spirituality

O God, who meets us where we are, leaving no one out, show
us clearly the path laid out for us. At the moment everything
is cloudy. In the midst of change we need the strength of your
Holy Spirit. Show us how we can help those in greatest need;
our world so needs you, and your love. Amen.

Helen Clark, Paisley

President of the British Methodist Conference:
Martyn Atkins

Vice-President:
Ruby Beech

Youth President:
Rob Redpath

Women's Network President:
Ruth Turner

General Secretary:
David Deeks

Assistant Secretary:
Ken Howcroft

Co-ordinating Secretaries:
Anthea Cox
David Gamble
Jonathan Kerry
Peter Sulston

Diaconal Order Warden:
Susan Jackson

Thy
mercy will
not fail us,
nor leave thy
work undone.

H&P 784

Day 2

Praying with Christians in West Africa

Praise to you, O Lord our God, for the voice of the prophets calling us to obedience, for the melody of the psalmist inviting us to praise, for the wisdom of the proverbs informing our conscience and for the record of salvation leading us to faith in your Son, our Saviour Jesus Christ. Amen.

Lancelot Andrewes, 1555-1626

The Gambia District

Chairman:
p Norman Grigg°

Mission Partners:
th Mark and Sarah Jason
and Abishek

Experience Exchange:
Claire Rawlinson

Scholarship Students:
Juliana Robinson
(in Ghana)
Lilian Owens (volunteer
at Corrymeela)

Sierra Leone

Methodist President:
Francis Nabieu

Mission Partners:
t Michael Tettey
m Joanna Tettey and
Joelle

Almighty God, we give you thanks for the way your Spirit is moving through the lives of your people in **the Gambia**. As the River Gambia flows through this country – sustaining life within and around it – so we pray that your Spirit will feed and water the Church in all the work being done in your name. We thank you for the Methodist clinics, for the nurses, for the Methodist schools and for the dedication of the teachers who often work in difficult conditions. We pray that in the dry and dusty places your life-giving Spirit will water and feed, enabling growth in this developing place. Amen.

Christine and Doug Baker, Former EEPs in the Gambia

We give thanks for the large numbers of key people in the Methodist Church **Sierra Leone** who have received training in leadership and administration from teams from the Cliff College International Learning Centre (CCILC).
We pray that they may be able to use this training in their own work and pass what they have learned on to others.
We pray for reconstruction work in Sierra Leone;
for the restoration of manses around the country;
for the Methodist Primary School in Kailahun fighting against encroachment on their land.
We give thanks for the commitment of former pupils of Methodist schools in helping to rebuild their old schools;
for the systematic rebuilding of schools under the supervision of the Methodist Development Department in the Eastern Region for children from all communities whether Christian, Muslim or Animist.

Father God, we hardly dare to come asking for your mercy on the mess we have made of your beautiful world. Forgive us that humankind everywhere worships money and power instead of worshipping you. Forgive us for the billions spent on war while our brothers and sisters cannot afford basic medicines. Lord, make your Church a beacon of hope and the leaven which transforms society, and by your grace and power make us part of that transformation.

Jennifer Gibson, Local Preacher, Worthing

Dublin District

Superintendent:
John Stephens

Loving Father, we thank you for the joy of knowing you and pray that the life of the Dublin District may reflect your love. We give thanks for the growth we have seen in our churches due to the influx of new residents from all over the world; for the diversity this has given us in our churches and the opportunity to learn from one another; for the way circuits are adapting to the new structures within Irish Methodism.
We pray that the District will continue to embrace changes within the city, will have a sense of vision and will seek to give witness in the new areas of growth and development.

John Stephens, Dublin District Superintendent

London District

Chair:
Ermal Kirby

Co-chairs:
Jenny Impey
Stuart Jordan

Give thanks for young people in our churches who are growing in their faith and in their willingness to share that faith with others.
Pray for our involvement in 'Listening to London'; for churches and projects seeking to adapt to changing needs and opportunities in our changing communities.

> Generous God,
> you offer us in Christ
> all that we need to fulfil our calling.
> In faith we ask
>   for wisdom to know your will
>   for strength and courage to do your will
>   for grace to show your love to all people.
> We ask this for your glory's sake. Amen.
>
> *Ermal Kirby, London District Chair*

the District Chairs have been walking the patch and 'listening to London'

Companions in faith
Caring
Omnipresent
Mighty
Patient God,
Always loving, you offer
New life through Jesus Christ your Son;
In you I put my trust, so that
On my journeying, I may be aware of the
Needs of those journeying alongside me,
So that together we may be
Companions in Faith. Amen.

Pam Turner, Connexional Women's Network President 2007-8

What joy the blest assurance gives, I know that my Redeemer lives!

H&P 196

11

Day 3

Praying with Christians in West Africa

Grant to us, Lord, the gift of inward happiness and the serenity that comes from living close to you. Renew in us each day the gift of joy that, bearing a good courage, we may meet what comes with a gallant heart, giving thanks to you in all things; through Christ our Lord. Amen.

Toc H Prayer

Bénin

Methodist President:
Simon Dossou

Scholarship Students:
Theophile Djekinnou°
(in Bénin)
Eli Tchekpo° (in Bénin)
Adolphe Zannou-Tchoko
(in Bénin)

Côte d'Ivoire

United Methodist Bishop:
Benjamin Boni

Togo

Methodist President:
Benjamin Gaba

*shore at Cotonou, Bénin
(Margaret Michelmore)*

Lord God, you gave life to all that is and you lead the world towards fulfilment in your kingdom; we adore and bless you.
We pray for the Church in the whole world,
that it may grow in truth and love;
for l'Église Protestante Méthodiste du **Bénin**.
By your grace, restore its unity and banish its transgressions;
for Bénin that the authorities may seek all that unites in justice and peace, and sustain their efforts for development;
for all those who suffer; we entrust them to your mercy.
Through Jesus Christ, your Son and our Saviour. Amen.

From prayers written by the Union of Methodist Men, Bénin

A prayer for reconciliation
O risen Saviour, who has reconciled humanity to God, you know the conflicts and divisions that exist in the world, and we think especially of those that divide families and churches. We pray for the Église Protestante Méthodiste du Bénin: guide the members in ways of reconciliation, and inspire and raise up ecumenical mediators once again for the total healing of our Church. Amen.

From prayers written by the Union of Methodist Women, Bénin

We give thanks for the Methodist witness for peace and reconciliation through the civil war and political conflict;
for the witness of the Church's worship and music.
We pray for the new medical project of EMUCI **Côte D'Ivoire** with the Texas Conference of UMC for women and children affected by malaria;
for the Revd Marcel Sachou as he leads the outreach of the Department of Evangelism and Missions in areas cut off during the war and among people whom the gospel has not yet reached;
for continued efforts in the country to negotiate effective instruments of government after the war.

Roy Crowder, Africa Secretary, WCO

South East District

Chair:
John Hellyer

We give thanks for opportunities to develop imaginative approaches to mission and to plan churches in areas of new housing.
We pray for the two circuits that have come together to form a new URC/Methodist United area in central Sussex;
for the work of the Kent Workplace Mission chaplaincy team in places such as the Bluewater Shopping centre as they continue to develop ways of supporting Christians at work;
for the BFree Youth Café and Information Centre in Leatherhead, a partnership between the churches and the local authority which provides a safe space for young people to meet;
for the assistant District Chairs, Mannie Jacob, Sheila Foreman and Peter Neatham;
for the Synod Secretary, David Ridley.

> We give praise to the Father
> who made all things.
> We give thanks to the Son
> who draws all people to himself.
> We open ourselves to the Spirit
> who makes all things new. Amen.
>
> *John Hellyer, South East District Chair*

John Wesley Primary School, which is currently being built in Ashford in the South East District.

Lord, who is part of every good resolve, I cannot reach all people, but let me speak your name in my own community, for you are there, in the streets and the shops, the blocks of flats and the housing estates, at the bus stops and in the workplaces. Help me to talk of you, especially to those who will despise me, and to do all these things in the strength of Jesus Christ. Amen.

Selwyn Veater, Prayer Co-ordinator, Brighton and Hove Circuit

May God grant us the vision to see
    beauty in the bleakest landscape
    truth in the most confusing of questions
    glimpses of holiness in the darkness of despair.
May God,
    the Weaver of Life,
    the Author of the Word
    and the Source of all Wisdom,
bless each one of us now and always. Amen.

Michaela Youngson,
Secretary for Pastoral Care and Spirituality

Be thou my vision, O Lord of my heart.

H&P 378

13

Day 4

Praying with Christians in West Africa

Lord, let nothing stand between us and your kingdom. May our souls be strengthened through our suffering, our lives clothed with your humility, and our desires purified by your holiness. As we show mercy may we receive it. As we embrace peace may we become your children and in our single-mindedness may we see you, face to face; through Christ our Lord. Amen.

Dorothy L. Sayers, 1893-1957

Equatorial Guinea

Methodist President:
Manuel Sañabá Silochi

Ghana

Methodist Presiding Bishop:
Robert Aboagye-Mensah

Scholarship Student:
Moses Agyam°
(in Britain)

We give thanks for the continued witness of the Methodist Church in **Equatorial Guinea** despite decades of isolation; for the willingness of the Methodist Church **Ghana** to support the future development of the Church.
We pray that the country's increasing oil profits may bring more benefits than curses to its people.

Roy Crowder, Africa Secretary, WCO

God bless Africa
God of our forebears, who has always been the shining light to our nations throughout the ages, you alone deserve praise and adoration because of your mighty works.
We pray for this great and rich continent of Africa;
that Africa may be healed of disease, poverty, hunger, HIV/AIDS, crime, unemployment and wars;
that the sons and daughters of this beloved continent may be richly blessed by your everlasting peace and harmony;
that all the nations of this continent may know you, trust you and worship you.
God bless Africa and all her children.
God bless the Church in Africa and guard her leaders.
God save Africa
and may his countenance forever shine upon her.
God bless Africa. Amen.

Gcobani Vika, Minister, Southern Africa

Heavenly Father, we thank you that you do not discriminate – teach us to do the same.
We have all sinned and fallen short of your glory – yet you still love us.
No one is outside of your love – you died that ALL our sins would be forgiven, you call us to repent and walk in your ways, to love as you love, in and through your strength and power. In these sad and difficult times, let us hear your call in our lives and respond to you and make this world a better place for all, to your praise and glory. Amen.

Eileen McDonald, Mission Partner, South Africa

Midlands and Southern District (Ireland)

Superintendent:
Paul Kingston

Give thanks that outreach in Kenmare, County Kerry, has led to the formation of a new Methodist Society in the town; for the 'Funky Fish Restaurant', a new drop-in centre in Bandon which is meeting a definite need.
We pray for the outreach work of the congregations in Killarney and Kenmare which has not had a Methodist minister for several years;
for the stationing process, that the right person may be found to nurture and expand the work;
for the Officers of the Youth and Children's Department of the Church as they appoint a resident Youth Development Worker in the Republic of Ireland.

Bedfordshire, Essex and Hertfordshire District

Chair:
Anne Brown

Bedfordshire, Essex and Hertfordshire District Candle

We give thanks for the work of the Church and Community Development Officer, Tony Barker, working with the Church of England, United Reformed Church and Methodist Churches across the areas of new housing in the East of England region.
We pray for youth workers working in churches, schools and communities;
for the Synod Secretary, Kathy Burrell;
for Richard Armiger, TDO, as he helps circuits undertake reviews; for his work with Local Preachers and the training events he facilitates across the District.

God of all good things, you invite us to share
    in the feast of life.
We thank you for everything
that attracts our eyes;
that delights our ears;
that touches our hearts.
Forgive us for not always sharing these
    good things with others.
Make us generous and open so that all may know
that you are the God of all good things.

Anne Brown, Bedfordshire, Essex and Hertfordshire District Chair

How marvellous you are, how wonderful your ways with humankind. Yours is a faithfulness that never changes, does not diminish with the passing years.
We can only marvel at your love for us expressed in Jesus Christ your Son. Amen.

John Lawley, Much Wenlock

God be
in my head,
and in my
understanding.

H&P 694

15

Day 5

Praying with Christians in West Africa

Holy God, too great to be trifled with and too wise to be deceived by insincerity; compose our thoughts as we enter your presence, order our minds as we bring our petitions, and grant us grace to offer you the loving sacrifice of hearts both steadfast and obedient; through Jesus Christ our Lord. Amen.

Susanna Wesley, 1669-1742

Cameroon

Moderator of the Presbyterian Church:
Nyansako-ni-Nku

Scholarship Students:
Divine Ekoko°
  (in South Africa)
Glory Befeke (Anye)°
  (in Britain)

Nigeria

Methodist Prelate:
Ola Makinde

Mission Partners:
m Hazel and Andrew
  Bryce (+CA)
p Ros Colwill
d Hans and Mary Van
  den Corput, Marcel and
  Maurice
p/ad Cecil Johnston (+CA)

Scholarship Students:
Jane Ameh (in Britain)
Evans Onyemara
  (in Britain)
Ministers' Group Training
  (in Nigeria)

Heavenly Father, we thank you for the country of **Cameroon**, for its peoples, its resources and the rich diversity of its cultures. We pray that you may guide its leaders in the ways of justice and of peace, heal its tribal and regional divisions, and draw its peoples increasingly into a living relationship with yourself. We pray particularly for our partner church, the Presbyterian Church in Cameroon, that you may sustain its institutions, deepen and strengthen the faith of its members, and give courage to its pastors as they proclaim your Word and seek the coming of your kingdom, through Jesus Christ our Lord. Amen.

Peter Ensor, former Mission Partner, Cameroon

Lord, we pray for **Nigeria**: many tribes and yet one nation;
for those who do good work and those who do wrong;
for those who share food and hospitality and those who have little;
for those who pray and fast;
for those who serve their fellow people;
for those who need encouragement, respect and love;
for the residents, patients and workers at the Amaudo Centres for the mentally ill;
for the Welfare Centre at Uzuakoli which is linked to those who have had leprosy;
for Ugwueke Hospital;
for those working at the Conference Office in Lagos;
for all those who try to serve the Lord.
Lord, meet their needs for we ask this in Jesus' name.
God is good! All the time! Amen? Amen!

Nigel Simpson, former Mission Partner, Nigeria

Eze family at Uzuakoli, Nigeria,
(Nigel Simpson)

We give thanks to God for all those people, lay and ordained, who exercise chaplaincy-style ministry in the mission life of the Church;
for standing with people in their everyday lives, listening, meeting, helping to make sense of life in our amazing world;
for telling the stories of those people and that world to the Church to shape our mission and ministry;
for the prophet voice calling all to the feast.
We pray for chaplains and the people they meet in places of work; shops, factories, retail parks, on the high street, in hospitals, universities and other places of education, entertainment centres and exhibition halls, the law courts, the armed forces, rural communities, residential homes, NCH projects and hospices.

Birmingham District
Chair:
Bill Anderson

Come,
diverse peoples,
each one unique,
in God's image made,
Jesus has prepared by grace a feast of love
and all are invited.

'I couldn't come, my life's a mess.'
'Me? I'm just a refugee.'
'I would never pass the test.'
'I'm not up to much.'
'I'm far too busy.'
'But you know about my lifestyle.'
'I limp and stutter and can't see.'
'Look at the colour of my skin, behind this veil.'
'Not me, I'm destitute.'
'I'm invisible, not even a number,
    you can't mean me.'

Come,
diverse peoples,
each one unique,
in God's image made,
Jesus has prepared by grace a feast of love
and all are invited,
even you,
and me. Amen.

Bill Anderson after Charles Wesley's
'Come, sinners to the gospel feast'.

Thy
sovereign
grace to all
extends.

H&P 46

Day 6

Praying with Christians in Southern Africa

Accept our thanks, O God, for the life that is within us, for the beauty that surrounds us and for the song of your creation. Receive our praise for the friends at our side, for the pleasures that abound and for the great work of our salvation, through your only begotten Son, our Saviour Jesus Christ. Amen.

John Baillie, 1886-1960

The Methodist Church in Southern Africa

Methodist Presiding Bishop:
Ivan Abrahams

South Africa

Mission Partner:
sd Eileen McDonald

Botswana

Lesotho

Mozambique

Namibia

Swaziland

Virgin and Child, Lesotho. (John Nutt)

We thank God for the work and mission of the Theological Education by Extension College (TEE) in **Southern Africa** over the last 30 years and for the work of TEE internationally. We pray for God's guidance for the new principal, Dr Tony Moodie, the staff in Johannesburg, and the Regional Co-ordinators, tutors and markers throughout the region. We pray for 3,000 students, 1,000 of whom are Methodist local preachers who will touch the lives of people, from remote villages to cosmopolitan cities. Amen.

Lynell Massey, Student Support Co-ordinator, TEE

Reach down and touch the lives of your suffering people. Anoint your Church as we minister in the name of Jesus. Protect all who work in **Namibia** and throughout Southern Africa. Bring healing and transformation to your people who suffer in the midst of poverty, disease and recovery from the effects of apartheid.

Isabel Stuart

Lord God, we give thanks for the people of **Swaziland**, particularly the people of Lomahasha village who raised funds, prayed and toiled for 10 long years to complete their new church to your glory. We pray for families in Swaziland destroyed by HIV/AIDS and for the projects providing care, food and education for orphaned children.
Help us, who have so much, to learn from the faithful people of Swaziland, who have so little and yet entrust themselves to your mighty protection. Amen.

Sue and Peter Finney, former EEPs Swaziland

God, our Father and Mother in heaven, we thank you for your blessings on the people of **Mozambique** thus far. We ask you to look with kindness and care on them, assure them of your love and healing ability in the midst of diseases like HIV/AIDS and malaria. Strengthen the leadership of the country and in a special way the leadership of the Church as they make sense of your word when faced with pain and suffering. Amen.

Bernardino Mandlate

We give thanks to God for the diversity of people within the congregations of the District;
for the rich relationships with, and between, asylum seekers and refugees;
for the growing number of lay appointments within the circuits;
for their impact on the Church's mission;
for those congregations that have re-established children's work, and for the part which children play within the worshipping community;
for those who respond to the challenge of becoming an inclusive Church that embraces children and young people.
We pray for the children, parents, staff, heads, governors and chaplains of the 11 Methodist and Methodist/Anglican primary schools within the District, praying especially for those schools in areas of economic and social deprivation;
for the work of the Queen's Hall, Wigan, giving thanks for new people in the congregation;
for the work of evangelism and caring for people in the name of Jesus, especially the new 'Bricklayer's Arms' responding to needy people in Wigan town centre;
for the new Rochdale and Littleborough circuit, that as the gifts of God's people are further discerned and shared, the ministry within the Circuit will flourish.

Bolton and Rochdale District

Chair:
David King

We thank you that in every generation your desire is to renew and revive your people. Give us the zeal that we often sing about, yet so often fail to put into practice. Grant to us the desire to witness to our faith, and serve each other through the power of your Holy Spirit. Make us humble and more effective in our discipleship. This we ask in the name of Jesus. Amen.

David King, Bolton and Rochdale District Chair

O God of unity and reconciliation, forgive our eager desire to find the beliefs, abilities and faults that divide us from others. Enable us to lay aside the trivial differences that separate us and discover afresh our common humanity. May we rejoice in the shared experiences of joy and sorrow, hope and despair, the weakness of the flesh and the exaltation of the Spirit within. May we know ourselves to be one with others in your world and in your presence. Through Christ our reconciling Lord. Amen.

Alan Taplin, Supernumerary Minister, Wigan

Blest be the dear uniting love, that will not let us part.

H&P 752

Day 7

Praying with Christians in Southern Africa

Praise to you, O Lord and our God, for the jewel of our sight, the treasure of our hearing, and the glory of our speech. Pardon our ingratitude and teach us to render you a thankful heart. Open our eyes to your glory, our ears to your word and our mouths to proclaim your goodness; now and forever. Amen.

Thomas Traherne, 1636-74

The United Church of Zambia

Synod Bishop:
Mutale Mulumbwa

Mission Partners:
s/d Jenny Featherstone
[+CofS]
th Colin Johnston
[+CofS]
p David° and Rhoda
Nixon, Samuel and
Christopher

Zimbabwe

Methodist Presiding Bishop:
Simbarashe Sithole

Mission Partners:
ed/sd Jonathan and
Isobel Hill, Stephen and
Susanna
rt Pat Ibbotson

Scholarship Students:
Simon Madhiba°
(in South Africa)
Allen Matsikiti°
(in Britain)
Walter Magagula°
(in Zimbabwe)

We pray for the staff and students of the UCZ Theological College, **Zambia**, especially its Principal, the Revd Dr Musonda Bwalya, and the Revd Colin Johnston, a mission partner, who lectures there;
for the Mindolo Training Farm, that its funding issues will be resolved so that training may be resumed;
and for children who drop out of school because they are required by their families to work in the fields or on commercial farms.
We give thanks for the work of Siby and Sofiya Tharakan who have been on the staff at MEF since March 2005, helping with IT and curriculum development and for the rapidly expanding work of the Theological Education by Extension in Zambia (TEEZ) .

We pray for the nine ministerial students and two diaconal students who have started their training programmes for the BTh/DipTh and Cert in Diaconal Ministry at the theological college in Zambia.

Musonda Bwalya, Principal

We pray for the Methodist Church in **Zimbabwe**, that it may be a Church that stands for life, peace, truth and justice;
for an end to the political and economic difficulties which are having a severe knock-on effect on the Church;
for the printing and book-binding business being run from the Connexional office to raise funds for the Church;
for the work of the Revd Margaret James in building up Theological Education by Extension for student ministers;
for the Matthew Rusike Children's Home, as more housing units are built and plans develop to open sister homes in both Bulawayo and Gweru.
We give thanks for Jonathan Hill who has been teaching at Thekwane High School for 21 years;
for his wife, Isobel, who is in charge of food distribution at the Hillside Methodist Church weekly feeding scheme;
and for the donors in the UK who fund most of the scheme.

Lakelands

Superintendent:
Kenneth Robinson

O God, we praise you for the beauty of your creation, and for the joy of beholding such a wonderful place. When we look at the lakes, we are reminded that Jesus is the Living Water, and when we see the mountains, we remember the Rock of Ages. Thank you for the stability you provide and the life you give every day. We ask you to draw near to the farming community who work long hours for diminishing returns. Give them your peace in their hearts. May large supermarkets be inspired to give fair prices for their produce and may government policies encourage more to work on the land. We pray that you will guide your ministers in the Lakelands to know how best to serve in such a large and rural District. May their ministry enable all to discover in Jesus the one who alone can give us security. We pray in his name. Amen.

Kenneth Robinson, Lakelands District Superintendent

Bristol District

Chair:
Ward Jones

Mission Partners:
Ose° and Jane°
  Barbarosa da Silva
  and Ose Junior (Brazil)

We give thanks for the team encouraging and nurturing fresh expressions of what it is to be church in the twenty-first century – David Bagwell, Mark Barrett, Rachel Borgars, Stephen Cullis, Susan Graham, Charity Hamilton, Cassandra Howes, Derrick Norton, Monica Sandy and Nicola Slateford; for over 250 people across the District who have taken up the challenge to bring a freshness to their current worship and mission or are investing in radical projects.

We pray for our circuits and United Areas as they consider their response to 'Reshaping for Misson' – a District-wide initiative designed to encourage creative thinking about the use of premises and financial and human resources;
for those considering how circuit boundaries might be redrawn to strengthen the effectiveness of the District's mission;
for the District Treasurer, Ian Robertson;
for the Complaints Officers, Elaine Gibson and Alan Hudson;
for the Complaints Panel Convenor, Paul Weir;
for the Deputy Chair, Peter Mortlock;
for the Lay Stationing Officer, Andrew Owen.

God of all,
when my world seems to be disintegrating around me
remind me that this is your world
and that through Christ
you are forever reconciling the world to yourself. Amen.

Alison Judd, Connexional Women's Network President 2005-6

Yours is the strength that sustains dedication.

H&P 700

21

Day 8

Praying with Christians in East Africa

O uncreated One, bless those whom you have made in your image. O untouchable One, draw near to us in the Word made flesh. O ineffable One, disclose yourself to us in the wisdom of the Cross. O immortal One, bring us through death to eternal life; through the same Christ our Lord. Amen.

Angela of Foligno, 1248-1309

Kenya (Tanzania and Uganda)

Methodist Presiding Bishop:
Stephen Kanyaru M'Impwii

Mission Partners:
n Barbara Dickinson
m Claudia Freund [+EMK]
n Jane Gray
ed Helen Moorehead
d Claire Smithson
sd Jeana Scofield

Experience Exchange:
Joanne Dolman

Scholarship Students:
Julius Kithinji° (in South Africa)
Patrick Muriungi° (in Britain)
Charles Ssebaggala (in Britain)
Isabiyre Harrington (in Malaysia)

We give thanks for the work of Helen Moorehead with the deaf in **Kenya**. We pray for the Kaaga School for the Deaf and for deaf children boarding at Marimanti Primary School in the Tharak District while a dedicated classroom and domitories are built.

Lord, make me a person of excellence,
one who is brightened by your radiance.
I am just some clay in your hand,
waiting for you to mould and
shape me into your desired form.
Till in Zion I finally lay it all down.

Teach me your word, O my Lord,
that I may walk in your righteous path,
narrow and trying as it may be.
Give me grace to claim and love it as my own.
Hold my hand and never let me go.
Till in Zion I finally lay it all down.

You are the great Shepherd of my soul
and in you I live and have my being.
Lead me graciously to your eternal rest
and as you lead, help me give my best
to you who died to set me free.
Till in Zion I finally lay it all down. Amen.

Margaret Wanjiru Kithinji,
Women's Fellowship Secretary, Methodist Church of Kenya

John Nutt

We give thanks for the dedicated women who uphold the witness of the Methodist Church in **Tanzania**.
We remember those who live in poor fishing villages along Lake Victoria around Musoma.
We praise God that they work with the little they have to make more to build the church in their community.

Roy Crowder, World Church Secretary, Africa

We give thanks for our increasingly diverse communities and especially for Christians from around the world who are joining Methodist congregations;
for the new opportunities in ministry offered to the Methodist Church in Wales by the new Synod structure* and for greater co-operation between circuits.
We pray for the new Synods and their officers as they explore new ways of working;
for the outreach ministry of deacons working in Swansea, Neath, Port Talbot, Cardiff, St Athan and Ynys Mon;
for Deacon Lorraine Brown, the new Director of the Amelia Trust Farm;
for our chaplains and especially Ian Waugh commencing agricultural chaplaincy in mid-Wales;
for the success of the new project in Powys;
for Sue Lawler and her family as she begins her ministry to the Welsh- and English-speaking churches;
for the Synod Enabler working with ethnic minority congregations.

Synod Cymru will care for the Welsh Language churches and the Wales Synod will care for the English Language churches throughout Wales.

Yr Eglwys Fethodistaidd yng Nghymru: The Methodist Church in Wales

Mission Partners:
Edson° and Sammire Dube, Nomthandozo and Nozipho (Zimbabwe)

Y Cyngor (The Council)

Synod Cymru
Chair: Patrick Slattery

Wales Synod
Chair: William Morrey
Chair: Stephen Wigley

> Come, sinners, to the gospel feast,
> Let every soul be Jesu's guest;
> You need not one be left behind,
> For God has bidden all mankind.
>
> Dowch, bechaduriaid, dowch i'r wledd,
> Mae'r Iesu'n cynnig ichwi hedd:
> Mae croeso i bawb i ddod at Dduw,
> Mae'r alwad i holl ddynol-ryw.

All things in Christ are ready now
Gracious God,
you have prepared for us in Christ
such good things as pass our understanding.
In those things for which we can make ready,
grant us vision;
in those things for which we cannot prepare,
grant us courage;
in those things which find us unready,
grant us the wisdom to trust and know that
'all things in Christ are ready now'.
We ask this in the power of his Spirit
and for the sake of his kingdom. Amen.

Will Morrey

the Sennedd (Welsh Assembly Building) and Millennium Centre where the 2007 Youth Conference will be hosted.

Here
for faith's
discernment
pray we.

H&P 616

23

Day 9

Praying with Christians in South America

Flood our lives with your grace, O Lord. Fill our whole being with your radiance, our innermost souls with your presence, and our very wills with your strength. Let us shine with the light of Christ, let us preach by example and let us carry nothing in our hearts but your love; through Christ our Lord. Amen.

John Henry Newman, 1801-90

Brazil
Methodist Bishop:
Joao Carlos Lopez

Experience Exchange:
Sandra Wilson

Uruguay
Methodist President:
Oscar Bolioli

Scholarship Student:
Mary Estefan (in Cuba)

Argentina
Methodist Bishop:
Nelly Ritchie

Mission Partner:
p Sue Jansen°

Colombia
Head of Church:
Juan Alberto Cardona

Scholarship Students:
Juan Guerrero°
  (in Colombia)
Ministers' group training
  (in Colombia)

Pray for schools in **Brazil**, that God will give wisdom to the head teachers so that they will lead according to his purposes. Pray for Brazilian Methodist pastors and their families; for joy and strength in their ministry. Amen.

Bishop Joao Carlos Lopez

Lord, give us the ability to understand that we are all your creatures and that we all live under the same grace. Deliver us from our divisions, and from feelings of being different and distant from one another. Destroy our arrogance so that we can meet as children of the same father. Give us the ability to open our minds so that we can understand your will as people and as faith communities. Give us the courage to become instruments of your will for a full life with justice and peace for all. Amen.

*Oscar Bolioli, President of the Methodist Church, **Uruguay***

Lord, we thank you for the security of your blessing in our lives. On many occasions we are running so fast that we don't pay attention to your presence on our path. We thank you for journeying with us. In **Argentina** many people are suffering and living without hope. Give us, O Lord, the power of your Spirit to preach the gospel, to speak your prophetic message, and to serve people with love in the secure knowledge that your kingdom will come. In the name of Jesus. Amen.

Bishop Aldo Etchegoyen, Secretary General, Council of Evangelical Methodist Churches of Latin America and the Caribbean

We pray to God that his kingdom may grow in **Colombia** and that there may be peace in this long-suffering and beaten country. We pray for the Colombian Methodist Church to develop ecclesiastically, physically and economically so that it can serve our God more and more every day. We pray for unity to prevail in our communities as well as in the whole of Colombia. May the Lord bless us with his power. Amen.

Bishop Juan Alberto Cardona, Methodist Church, Colombia

We give thanks for the diverse communities of the Cumbria District; its scattered rural villages, market towns and its urban centres in Carlisle, Barrow-in-Furness and along the west coast;

for the richness of landscape, culture and heritage enjoyed by many millions of visitors;

for the vital witness of Christians, often in small membership churches, who celebrate God's love and offer worship, prayer and a caring ministry in their local communities.

We pray for 'Into Life', a district project to encourage the development of a renewed learning culture among Methodists;

for young families, low-waged and migrant workers unable to afford local housing;

for ecumenical and secular partnerships tackling climate change, social cohesion, domestic violence, energy issues and for initiatives to reduce re-offending.

Generous God,
you give yourself to us in Christ,
you give us to each other in Christ;
in the love of Christ
give us to the world and to its people. Amen.

David Emison, Cumbria District Chair

Cumbria District

Chair:
David Emison

Churches in Cumbria work with partners in 'The Sustainable Communities' project

A blessing
God of the poor,
bless us with your compassion.
God of the bereaved,
bless us with your comfort.
God of the humble,
bless us with gentleness.
God of the righteous,
bless us with wisdom.
God of the merciful,
bless us with forgiveness.
God of the pure in heart,
bless us with kindness.
God of the peacemakers,
bless us with understanding.
God of the persecuted,
bless us with courage. Amen.

© Stella Bristow, Witney and Faringdon Circuit, from 'Sensing God' published by Inspire

Blest be the tie that binds our hearts in Jesu's love.

H&P 754

25

Day 10

Praying with Christians in South America

To you, O Lord, let us direct our eyes.
To you let us offer our hands.
To you let us bow the knee.
To you let us sacrifice our life.
To you let us come at the last
and in you let us rest for ever. Amen.

Walter Raleigh, 1552-1618 (attributed)

Bolivia
Methodist Bishop:
Carlos Poma

Scholarship Student:
Reynaldo Pontillo
(in Brazil)

Chile
Methodist Bishop:
Neftalí Aravena Bravo

Mission Partner:
p/sd Alison Facey°, Chris
Esdaile, Luke and
Bethan

Peru
Methodist Bishop:
Jorge Bravo Cabellero

rt Margaret° and Aldo
Valle

Ecuador
Methodist Bishop:
Salomón Cabezas

We pray for the Methodist Church in **Bolivia** as it works out a new projection of its mission, vision and structure approaching its next centenary;
for leaders who work in councils and in government departments, that they may be the salt and light of God's presence;
for those affected by the floods and the frost in the Altiplano;
for the process of drafting a new constitution;
for President Evo Morales in his commitment to rule as a father;
for those in need who were forgotten for over 500 years;
for the indigenous people in their awakening and construction of the great pachakuti (transformation) of *suma qamaña* (being and well-being) so that we can all live in harmony.

Bishop Carlos Poma, Bishop of Bolivia

Life-giving God, source of all love, your energy and creative Spirit fill the earth! Through you we dare to hope for a *fiesta* in which all people will join; with you we dare to search for a song to be sung by the whole earth; in you we dare to dream of the liberation which Christ has promised. Amen.

*Chris Esdaile, Mission Partner, **Chile***

Dear Lord, we thank you for being with the Methodist Church in **Peru**. May your gospel reach the Peruvian government and people. We pray for children, young people with no education, the poor and marginalised, women who have been abandoned, the elderly and those infected with HIV. May your grace be with us. Amen.

Bishop Jorge Bravo Caballero, Bishop of Peru

We pray for the God of love and grace to have mercy on the people of **Ecuador**, guiding the President and his government to fight tirelessly against corruption and against those who stand in the way of integrity. We pray for the development of programmes of integral evangelism with all the members of our Methodist churches. With the blessing of Our Lord Jesus Christ we will prosper.

Bishop Salomon Cabezas, Bishop of Ecuador

We give thanks for prayer rooms set up every circuit across the North West District as part of the 24/7 prayer initiative; for 175 years of life and witness of the Ardara church in South West Donegal.
We pray for the future of the second prison in Northern Ireland located at Magilligan, as relocation is being discussed; for rural communities at a time when the suicide rate is rising.

North West District (Ireland)

Superintendent:
Harold Agnew

Give thanks for churches that are introducing new and fruitful patterns of Sunday worship and youth work; for the growing work of Methodist Homes.
Pray for those employed in the finance industry, that they may be diligent, honest and eager to encourage a just use of resources;
for an awareness of the rich Methodist heritage in the Channel Islands and the courage to offer the gospel in our changing culture;
for the Church as it continues to offer hospitality and friendship to visitors and to the many nationalities who have made these islands their home;
for the work of Stephen Robinson, the District's Synod Secretary.

Lord God, we thank you for calling us into the company of those who trust in Christ. May the roots of our life together draw refreshment from your life-giving Spirit and the fruits of our life of love come to be shared by all in the banquet of your kingdom.

David Coote, Channel Islands District Chair

Father, whose wisdom is wider than the horizons visible from the islands, whose love is deeper than the sea that surrounds them, and whose grace encompasses the traditions and history that make the islands unique, give to the Methodist people a vision, that we may be part of your plan for the Channel Islands.

David Hart, Superintendent, Guernsey

Channel Islands District

Chair:
David Coote

Freedom Tree, St Helier, Jersey. This bronze sculpture represents freedom, peace and hope for the future.

Lord, when I am tempted to hold on
to what I think is mine,
to my way of doing things,
to my security blankets;
help me to let go enough to discover that
in Christ, all things are possible. Amen.

Alison Judd, Connexional Women's Network President 2005-6

We have an anchor that keeps the soul steadfast and sure.

H&P 689

Day 11

Praying with Christians in Central America

Let us love you, O God, with a heart that you have made for yourself, with a mind that you alone can satisfy, with a soul that longs for your presence and with a strength spent in serving you all our days. Usurp our hearts, fill our minds, lift our souls and be our strength, now and for ever. Amen.

Walter Howard Frere, 1863-1938

Belize and Honduras District of the MCCA

District President:
David Goff

Mission Partner:
p Janet Corlett°
sd Maggie Patchett

Panama and Costa Rica District of the MCCA

District President:
Danoval Johnson

Guyana District of the MCCA

District President:
Barrington Litchmore

Scholarship Student:
Marc Piggott (in Jamaica)

Guatemala

Methodist President:
Tomás Riquiac Ixtán

Mexico

Methodist Bishop:
Moises Valderrama Gomez

We give thanks for Mrs Elswith Clare, the first candidate for the diaconal ministry accepted by the **Belize/Honduras** District in many years. We pray that there will soon be many more candidates. We give thanks for the Commissioned Lay Workers and pray particularly for those working as full-time pastors in the emerging Spanish-speaking congregations in Honduras.

Janet Corlett, Mission Partner, Bay Islands, Honduras

We pray to God for peace in Central America;
for the migratory situation between countries in the same region;
for the new local churches.

Bishop Fernando Palomo,
*Evangelical Methodist Church, **Costa Rica***

We pray for an improvement to the worrying social situation in **Guatemala**. Crime and violence are, as David said, our daily and nightly bread; too much death on our streets, too many killings of women. A lot of youngsters are involved in groups of organized crime, especially those who live in extreme poverty in exchange for inadequate pay. Let us pray for the Church to be a voice of hope and an instrument for evangelism and for the rehabilitation of those who are involved in evil crimes in exchange for money.

Tomas Riquiac Ixtan,
President of the Primitive Methodist Church, Guatemala

We pray to God for the street children of **Mexico** who are the victims of unjust exploitation;
for the women of Ciudad Juárez who are threatened and murdered every day;
for an end to crime and instability in Mexico due to violence and drug trafficking;
for young people drawn into the world of drugs;
for the indigenous peoples living in extreme poverty;
for our church to continue to establish the kingdom of God.

Bishop Jaime Vasquez

Give thanks for the growth of honest and inclusive Christian conversation in the book review meetings and café church at Chester, on circuit walks and wayside prayers at Winsford, country church theological 'chats' at Leek, and social encounters at the Potter's House and Oasis centres at Burslem Mission. We pray for the Fairtrade outlets at the Methodist Book Centre (Hanley) and 'Wesley' Chester; for the work of the churches' Link Officer in Stoke-on-Trent encouraging the city council in projects of social and urban renewal; for the work of Hazel Griffiths, the District Administrator.

Chester and Stoke-on-Trent District

Chair:
John Walker

Mission Partners:
Jimione° and Miriama Kaci, and Salanieta (Fiji)

Prayer of living in the all in all
Cosmic Christ, Galactic Lord,
your love draws a universal circumference.
Expand our minds,
enlarge our hearts,
excite our spirits
that we may flourish in freedom
within the safe orbit of your love.
Specific Spirit, Focused Presence,
your care lights on our inner moods and needs.
Inform our prayer,
inspire our hope,
inflame our love,
that we may find the Omega point within
where earth and heaven blend and meet. Amen.

John Walker, Chester and Stoke-on-Trent District Chair

60th anniversary celebrations of the Methodist Book Centre in Hanley, Stoke-on-Trent.

Shopping crowds in the popular centre of Chester are ministered to from the nearby Wesley Church with its city-centre ministry including a café church

---

Web of faith,
twined in thorns of uncertainty;
torn by wind and bitten by rain;
craving safe anchorage;
and praying to be firm rooted,
but praying in vain.
And yet hope
indefinable;
a fragile gossamer possibility.
Slender rope
holds life together all the while,
so I can confident be. Amen.

Wesley Blakey, Nottingham and Derby District Chair

In heaven
and earth
your folk
are one.

H&P 650

29

Day 12

Praying with Christians in the Caribbean

Jesus, by your wounded feet direct our path. Jesus, by your nailed hands move us to deeds of love. Jesus, by your pierced side purify our desires. Jesus, by your crown of thorns annihilate our pride. Jesus, by your broken heart, knit ours to yours. Amen.

Richard Crawshaw, 1613-49

Methodist Church in the Caribbean and the Americas (MCCA)

Connexional President:
George Mulrain

Scholarship Student:
Karen Durant° (in Britain)

Leeward Islands District of the MCCA

District President:
Franklyn Manners

South Caribbean District of the MCCA

District President:
Victor Job

Prayer for the MCCA's 40th anniversary of autonomy
Creator God, we are grateful for all those men and women who have piloted MCCA along the route of independence. We give thanks that the Church has been able to embrace so many mission opportunities. We ask you to help the Church resolutely to move forward on another forty years' journey and address more areas of need. We thank you for the blessing of ecumenical partnerships that have facilitated a better response to mission challenges within the Caribbean and the Americas and for the continuing links with sister churches in Britain, Canada, the United States and Latin America. Amen.

George Mulrain, MCCA Connexional President

Prayer for Antigua
God, our Redeemer, who inspired Nathaniel Gilbert, John Baxter and Thomas Coke to witness to your love in the island of Antigua, help us to use their examples as a stepping-stone for our own faith. We remember the Black Caribbean slaves, Bessie, Sophie, Mary Alleyn and Black Harry, who proclaimed your gospel in their daily lives. Help us to work for the freedom of all God's people and fire us with your Holy Spirit, that through prayer our faith may be strengthened.

Sandra Lewer, Connexional Women's Network President, 2006-7

Prayer for the start of the day
Be with me, dear God, throughout this day. I rejoice because Jesus Christ your Son has already set fine examples of how to relate in love to the people I will meet. I feel confident, knowing that the Holy Spirit will be ever-present to offer me guidance even as my many duties and challenges confront me. Grant that, throughout the waking hours of this day, my lips, hands, feet and, indeed, my whole self will offer you the worship and praise that you deserve. When I complete the day's tasks and eventually lie down to sleep, satisfy me with the knowledge that I have been a faithful child of yours. This I humbly pray. Amen.

George Mulrain, MCCA Connexional President

Give thanks for the creativity of churches throughout Cornwall as they continue to seek new ways of witness and worship in a changing society, including 'tubestation', a new and exciting project working in the surfing community at Polzeath on the North Cornwall coast.

Pray for all who offer their time, energy and gifts in the work of the Church throughout Cornwall;

for our District Lay Workers, both paid and voluntary, who are involved in work with children and young people, in community projects and in evangelism;

for the work of the recently-formed District Review Group as it considers how best to focus the mission and ministry of the District.

God of creation,
giver of life,
source in Christ of all things needful,
as the waters embrace all lands on this one planet,
so may your love embrace all nations as one;
as the winds sweep across the continents
to move and to shape this earth into its complex wholeness,
so may your energy sweep across all countries
to change and to form all peoples into a unified completeness;
as the sun emits light and warmth to all corners of the world,
so may your presence radiate hope and peace to all races.
Amen.

Ian Haile

Cornwall District

Chair:
Christopher Blake

Tubestation workers ministering to the surfing community at Polzeath.
© tubestation.org

Lord, teach me to find space
even in the hubbub and turmoil of my daily life,
to discover moments of tranquillity
in the most unlikely of places.
Help me to transform
the frustration of a traffic queue,
standing at the checkout
and waiting for my turn in the doctor's surgery
into an oasis of stillness within
as I allow Christ
to be all things
and in all places
to me. Amen.

David Clowes, Minister, Wigan Circuit
This prayer will appear in David's book '500 more prayers for Special Occasions' to be published by Kingsway in 2008.

A little
longer,
let us
linger still.

H&P 158

Day 13

Praying with Christians in the Caribbean

O Christ, the Good Shepherd, let us heed your voice. O Christ of the storm, bid us come to you unafraid upon the water. O Christ the Light, let us trust you in the darkness of our journey. O Christ, the Bread of Life, feed us in the desert places, now and for ever. Amen.

Bede Jarrett, 1881-1934

Jamaica District of the MCCA

District President: Byron Chambers

Bahamas and Turks and Caicos Islands District of the MCCA

District President: Raymond Neilly

Mission Partners:
p Eddie° and Susan Sykes, Jonathan and Thomas

Haiti District of the MCCA

District President: Raphael Dessieu

Cuba

Methodist Bishop: Ricardo Pereira Díaz

Scholarship Students: Cuba Group Training (in Cuba)

Dear God of Love,
we thank you for creating us in your image and likeness,
for the love displayed in the nature of our creation,
and in the many gifts we have received.
Although our abilities may be different, you have enabled
us to do what is required for others to experience your love.
We come with our weakness, seeking your strength.
We thank you that we can confess our sins to you
and ask for your forgiveness. We are sorry for our wrongdoing.
We pray for wisdom to understand what we should do
in situations in life, and for strength to do it correctly.
We thank you that we are allowed to speak to you
and to receive your loving response to our requests.
In the name of Jesus we pray. Amen.

*Constance Magnus, **Jamaica***

We pray for a strengthening of the mainstream churches in the **Bahamas** as TV evangelists become increasingly popular. Some of them preach irresponsibly and persuade followers to donate large sums of money which do not always go to charitable purposes.
We pray for the All Saints Community. Many of the residents are HIV positive and some have AIDS, or are homeless.
We give thanks for the expanding ministry of the John Wesley Methodist College (JWMC) and for the implementation of the Disciple programme, a resource for enabling people to understand the Bible and how it applies to the life of discipleship.

We pray that God will guide the people of **Puerto Rico** in the pursuit of political and social solutions to the climate of violence and social disintegration in the country. We pray that the Methodist Church in Puerto Rico will be an instrument of reconciliation, enlightenment and peace for all the different sections of the country. We remember the Latin American Council of Methodist Churches (CIEMAL) in our prayers. Amen.

Bishop Juan Vera, Bishop, Methodist Church, Puerto Rico

Prayer of thanksgiving

Heavenly Father, we worship you as the creator and sustainer
of the universe and we praise you for the gift of life, health
and strength.
Lord Jesus, we worship you, Saviour and Lord of the world
and we praise you for finding us, washing us, forgiving us
and giving us a place in your Church.
Holy Spirit, we worship you, Sanctifier of the people of God
and we praise you for renewing us and gifting us.
Glory to the Father, and to the Son, and to the Holy Spirit
as it was in the beginning, is now, and will be forever. Amen.

We pray that, as the North East District continues to implement
the 'Connexions' programme*, it may not be just about
structural change but also renewal for mission and service;
that our people would reach out to all with the good news of
Jesus Christ's grace and power.

an Ireland-wide restructuring programme to equip the Church for mission.

North East District (Ireland)

Superintendent:
Aian Ferguson

We give thanks for the imaginative work with young
skateboarders at Elm Ridge Church, Darlington;
for small village chapels seeking a new vision and mission for
the future.
We pray for the new United North East Circuit, uniting three
circuits in mission and service in Hartlepool, Peterlee and the
surrounding area of small ex-mining communities;
for the drop-in at Avenue Church in Middlesbrough and
Eston Circuit, offering a safe place of welcome and practical,
emotional and spiritual support to refugees and those
seeking asylum, who are often traumatized by the events
that caused them to leave their own countries, and some by
their treatment in this country;
for the Revd Rosa Leto, part-time workplace chaplain, in her
work in two Asda stores and a power station.

Darlington District

Chair:
Graham Carter

Welcoming God, in Christ you give
healing to the broken,
hope to the sorrowful,
comfort to the lonely,
new life to all.
Help us not to be too proud
to accept all that you offer us.

Richard Bielby, Acting Chair, Darlington District 2006-7

He
bids us
build each
other up.

H&P 753

Day 14

Praying with Christians in North America

Lord, let us be alert to you in the silence of our hearts. Let us be host to you in our homes. Let us discern you in our deeds of compassion. Let us welcome you in the guest at our table. Let us receive you in the intimacy of the upper room and finally let us behold you in the glory of your kingdom; through Christ our Lord. Amen.

Evelyn Underhill, 1875-1941

United Methodist Church (USA)
Ecumenical Officer to the Council of Bishops
William Oden

The United Church of Canada
General Secretary:
Jim Sinclair

'How many more senseless deaths will have to be counted before we enact meaningful firearms control in this country?'

The Revd Bob Edgar,
a United Methodist pastor
and leader of the National
Council of Churches

'We look to you, Jesus, to help us forgive what seems to be unforgivable.'

Deb Spaulding,
Faith United Methodist Church,
St Charles, Missouri.

Dear Lord, we pray for the people of the **United States** as they approach presidential elections in 2008; for the United Methodist Church as they meet for the General Conference. Help the UMC to organize itself so that its churches throughout the world can meet and focus on the challenges and joys closer to their cultural reality and specific socio-political situations, while affirming the unique global connexion that United Methodists have.

We give thanks for UMCOR, the relief agency of the United Methodist Church and for all the work it has been able to do ministering to the needs of people whose lives continue to be affected by Hurricane Katrina.

We remember 33 people killed at Virginia Tech on 16 April 2007 and pray for your comfort for their friends and families. We pray that some good may come of this tragedy: let it precipitate a sensible discussion on the balance between the right to bear arms and the need to protect society.

God of all creation, we offer you our thanksgiving for a time rich with connections, among each other and with you.
We thank you for moments when we have experienced what it is to be united, even in our differences.
Help us to grow as a listening, discerning, learning people.
Help us to give up patterns and structures that enslave us and others. Help us to acknowledge our fear and lean into your hope and your courage. Help us to grow in our trust in each other and in your Spirit.
Fill us with your grace and with your wisdom,
with your patience and with your love.
Propel us into your future,
rooted in the richness of our past.
In Christ we pray. Amen.

*A prayer from 'Call to Purpose: A message from the Church to the Church' , affirmed by the United Church of **Canada**'s 39th General Council meeting in Thunder Bay 2006.*

Give thanks for the changes and challenges we face as new circuits are created and resources more widely shared:
We pray that we will make the most of the opportunities that arise as thousands of new homes are built in this region;
for fresh enthusiasm in sharing our faith with others;
for the work of the Synod Secretary, Grahame Lindsay, and the Training & Development Officer, Jack Lawson.

Emmaus collect (Luke 24.13-35)
Lord Jesus Christ,
companion and interpreter,
as stranger and friend
you match your pace to ours upon the road,
bringing questions and answers,
discomfort and reassurance,
promise and potential.
Walk with us always, we pray,
unravelling mystery,
revealing truth
and breaking bread;
until our eyes are fully opened to your presence
and our burning hearts inflamed by your precious love. Amen.

Val Ogden, Director,
Selly Oak Centre for Mission Studies, The Queen's Foundation

East Anglia District

Chair:
Graham Thompson

Mission Partners:
Frank° and Gabi Aichele
(Germany)

the road to Emmaus © Gisele Bauche, used with permission

Father, creator and sustainer, we rejoice that in Christ our Saviour, you make all things
 one
 new
 just
 eternal
 loving
forgive the ways in which we live as though we do not know Christ and continue in
 disunity
 old ways
 injustice
 pragmatism
 violence
grant us a fresh vision of all that Christ offers, so that we may become more like him each day. Amen.

Graham Thompson, East Anglia District Chair

And we
the life
of God shall
know, for God
is manifest
below.

H&P 109

35

Canticle of Brother Sun

By St Francis of Assisi
translated for MPH by Primavera Quantrill

Monday

Altissimu, onnipotente bon Signore,
Tue so' le laude, la gloria e l'honore et onne benedictione.
Ad Te solo, Altissimo, se konfano,
et nullu homo ène dignu te mentovare.

Our Lord most high, almighty and good, yours be the praise,
the glory, honour and every blessing.
To you alone, O most high, are they due, and no man is
worthy to speak your name.

Tuesday

Laudato sie, mi' Signore cum tucte le Tue creature,
spetialmente messor lo frate Sole,
lo qual è iorno, et allumini noi per lui.
Et ellu è bellu e radiante cum grande splendore:
de Te, Altissimo, porta significatione.

Yours be the praise, my Lord, through all your creation,
especially Brother Sun, who is day and shines upon us.
Beautiful, radiant and filled with great splendour, he speaks to
us of your greatness.

Wednesday

Laudato si', mi Signore, per sora Luna e le stelle:
in celu l'ài formate clarite et pretiose et belle.

Yours be the praise, my Lord, for sister moon and the stars
in the heavens, for you have made them brilliant, precious
and beautiful.

Lectionary Readings and Psalms

This table of readings and psalms (Ps) is largely based on the Sunday themes of the Revised Common Lectionary and has been prepared by Norman Wallwork. Major holy days and special days of prayer and observation have been included.

For a daily reflection and commentary on the readings visit
www.methodistchurch.org.uk

Week beginning 2 September
22nd in Ordinary Time
Pride and Humility

S	2	Luke 14.1,7-14	Ps 81
M	3	Isaiah 2.5-17	Ps 119.65-72
T	4	Isaiah 57.14-21	Ps 17
W	5	Luke 14.15-24	Ps 15
T	6	2 Chronicles 12.1-12	Ps 113
F	7	Hebrews 13.7-21	Ps 112
S	8a	Luke 1.39-47	Ps 45

[a=Nativity of Blessed Virgin Mary]

Week beginning 9 September
23rd in Ordinary Time
Obedient Faith

S	9b	Luke 14.25-33	Ps 139
M	10	Genesis 39.1-23	Ps 101
T	11	2 Kings 2.1-12	Ps 24
W	12	Luke 18.18-30	Ps 125
T	13	Deuteronomy 7.12-26	Ps 127
F	14c	Philippians 2.5-11	Ps 22
S	15	Hebrews 5.1-10	Ps 110

[b=Racial Justice Sunday; c=Holy Cross Day]

Week beginning 16 September
24th in Ordinary Time
Relenting and Repenting

S	16	Luke 15.1-10	Ps 40
M	17	Amos 7.1-6	Ps 38
T	18	Jonah 3.1-10	Ps 39
W	19	Luke 22.54-62	Ps 130
T	20	Job 40.1-14	Ps 37.31-41
F	21d	Matthew 9.9-13	Ps 19
S	22	Hosea 11.1-12	Ps 25

[d=Matthew, Apostle]

Week beginning 23 September
25th in Ordinary Time
Oppression and Justice

S	23	Luke 16.1-13	Ps 79
M	24	Proverbs 14.12-31	Ps 80
T	25	Luke 20.45-21.4	Ps 82
W	26	Proverbs 17.1-5	Ps 86
T	27	Exodus 23.1-9	Ps 88
F	28	2 Corinthians 8.1-9	Ps 12
S	29e	John 1.47-51	Ps 69

[e=Michael and All Angels]

Week beginning 30 September
26th in Ordinary Time
Closing the Gap

S	30	Luke 16.19-31	Ps 97
M	1	Proverbs 22.2-16	Ps 108
T	2	Proverbs 28.3-10	Ps 57
W	3	Luke 9.43b-48	Ps 73.14-28
T	4	Ezekiel 18.5-24	Ps 10
F	5	Revelation 3.14-22	Ps 11
S	6	Amos 5.18-24	Ps 29

Week beginning 7 October
27th in Ordinary Time
Saving Faith

S	7	Luke 17.5-10	Ps 37
M	8	2 Kings 18.1-8, 28-36	Ps 15
T	9	2 Kings 19.8-20, 35-37	Ps 17
W	10	Matthew 20.29-34	Ps 27
T	11	Isaiah 7.1-9	Ps 46
F	12	Revelation 2.12-29	Ps 25
S	13	Romans 1.16-17	Ps 130

[Week of Prayer for World Peace]

Week beginning 14 October
28th in Ordinary Time
Healing Faith

S	14	Luke 17.11-19	Ps 28
M	15	Numbers 12.1-15	Ps 31.1-16
T	16	Leviticus 14.33-53	Ps 34
W	17	Luke 5.12-16	Ps 37.1-17
T	18f	2 Timothy 4.5-17	Ps 145
F	19	2 Timothy 2.1-7	Ps 42
S	20	James 5.13-18	Ps 44.16-27

[One World Week; f=Luke the Evangelist]

Week beginning 21 October
29th in Ordinary Time
Wrestling Faith

S	21	Luke 18.1-8	Ps 48
M	22	Genesis 32.22-31	Ps 50.1-15
T	23	Luke 11.5-13	Ps 55.1-12
W	24	Luke 22.39-46	Ps 55.13-17
T	25	Isaiah 54.11-17	Ps 55.18-26
F	26	2 Timothy 2.14-26	Ps 56
S	27	Micah 6.6-8	Ps 146

Week beginning 28 October
30th in Ordinary Time
A Kingdom of Justice

S	28	Luke 18.9-14	Ps 57
M	29g	John 15.17-27	Ps 19
T	30	Daniel 5.1-31	Ps 51
W	31	Luke 1.46-55	Ps 61
T	1h	Revelation 7.9-17	Ps 24
F	2	2 Timothy 2.1-10	Ps 63
S	3	Habakkuk 3.17-19	Ps 66

[g=Simon and Jude, Apostles-trans;
h=All Saints' Day]

Week beginning 4 November
31st in Ordinary Time
The Returning Sinner

S	4i	Luke 19.1-10	Ps 67
M	5	Amos 5.12-24	Ps 68.1-13
T	6	Zechariah 7.1-14	Ps 68.27-35
W	7	Luke 19.11-27	Ps 69.1-13
T	8	Proverbs 15.8-11, 24-33	Ps 70
F	9	Jude 5-21	Ps 71.1-13
S	10	Revelation 2.8-11	Ps 71.14-24

[i=Methodist Homes Sunday]

Week beginning 11 November
32nd in Ordinary Time
The Redeemer Lives

S	11j	Matthew 25.14-30	Ps 90
M	12	Job 19.23-27a	Ps 81
T	13	Revelation 1.12-18	Ps 84
W	14	Revelation 21.1-7	Ps 85
T	15	Exodus 3.13-20	Ps 86
F	16	Acts 24.10-23	Ps 89.1-18
S	17	Colossians 1.15-20	Ps 122

[j=Remembrance Sunday]

Week beginning 18 November
33rd in Ordinary Time
Solemn Warnings

S	18	Luke 21.5-19	Ps 89.19-37
M	19	1 Samuel 28.3-19	Ps 89.38-52
T	20	Jeremiah 17.14-18	Ps 90
W	21	Luke 17.20-37	Ps 91
T	22	Ezekiel 10.1-19	Ps 92
F	23	2 Thessalonians 1.3-12	Ps 93
S	24	Isaiah 12	Ps 141

[Prisons' Week]

Week beginning 25 November
Week before Advent
Christ the King

S	25k	Luke 23.33-43	Ps 45
M	26	Isaiah 52.13-53.12	Ps 22
T	27	Ezekiel 34.20-31	Ps 24
W	28	Luke 18.15-17	Ps 46
T	29	Isaiah 33.17-22	Ps 47
F	30lm	Matthew 4.18-22	Ps 28
S	1	John 21.24-35	Ps 97

[k=Christ the King & Youth Sunday;
l=Andrew, Apostle; m=World AIDS Day]

Week beginning 2 December
1st of Advent
The Approaching Salvation

S	2	Matthew 24.36-44	Ps 124
M	3	Genesis 6.11-22	Ps 98
T	4	Genesis 8.1-19; 9.8-13	Ps 122
W	5	Matthew 24.23-35	Ps 9.1-11
T	6	Isaiah 54.4-10	Ps 50.1-15
F	7	Hebrews 11.1-7, 32-40	Ps 21
S	8n	Romans 13.11-14	Ps 148

[n=Conception of Blessed Virgin Mary]

Week beginning 9 December
2nd of Advent
The Way of the Lord

S	9	Matthew 3.1-12	Ps 72
M	10	Isaiah 24.1-16a	Ps 82
T	11	Isaiah 40.1-11	Ps 94
W	12	Matthew 12.33-37	Ps 48
T	13	Genesis 15.1-18	Ps 67
F	14	Acts 13.16-33a	Ps 21
S	15	Isaiah 65.17-25	Ps 76

Week beginning 16 December
3rd of Advent
Healing in the Wilderness

S	16	Matthew 11.2-11	Ps 146
M	17	Isaiah 29.17-24	Ps 7
T	18	Ezekiel 47.1-12	Ps 24
W	19	Matthew 8.14-17, 28-34	Ps 43
T	20	Zechariah 8.1-17	Ps 25
F	21	Acts 5.12-16	Ps 53
S	22	Isaiah 44.1-8	Ps 80

Week beginning 23 December
4th of Advent
The Birth of the Messiah

S	23	Matthew 1.18-25	Ps 80
M	24	Isaiah 9.2-7	Ps 96
T	25o	Luke 2.1-20	Ps 85
W	26p	Acts 6.1-7	Ps 13
T	27q	John 13.21-35	Ps 92
F	28r	Jeremiah 31.15-17	Ps 124
S	29	John 1.1-14	Ps 110

[o=Christmas Day; p=Stephen, Martyr; q=John, Evangelist; r=Holy Innocents]

Week beginning 30 December
1st of Christmas
The Name above all Names

S	30	Luke 2.15-21	Ps 105
M	31	Philippians 2.5-11	Ps 98
T	1s	Luke 2.15-21	Ps 8
W	2	Galatians 4.4-7	Ps 123
T	3	Matthew 1.18-21	Ps 124
F	4	Hebrews 2.10-18	Ps 125
S	5	Titus 2.11-14	Ps 126

[s=Naming & Circumcision of Jesus]

Week beginning 6 January
The Epiphany
A Light to the Nations

S	6t	Matthew 2.1-12	Ps 72
M	7	Micah 5.2-9	Ps 27
T	8	Ephesians 3.14-21	Ps 131
W	9	Luke 13.31-35	Ps 132
T	10	1 Kings 10.1-13	Ps 45
F	11	1 Kings 10.14-25	Ps 133
S	12	Ephesians 1.3-14	Ps 147

[t=Epiphany & Covenant Sunday]

Week beginning 13 January
1st after Epiphany
A Servant Community

S	13u	Matthew 3.13-17	Ps 29
M	14	Genesis 35.1-15	Ps 42
T	15	Jeremiah 1.4-10	Ps 130
W	16	Matthew 12.15-21	Ps 43
T	17	Isaiah 51.7-16	Ps 46
F	18v	Acts 8.4-13	Ps 48
S	19	Romans 6.3-5	Ps 68.14-23

[u= Baptism of Christ; v=Octave of Prayer for Christian Unity begins]

Week beginning 20 January
2nd in Ordinary Time
The Saving Lamb

S	20	John 1.29-42	Ps 40
M	21	Exodus 12.1-28	Ps 54
T	22	Isaiah 52.13-53.12	Ps 66
W	23	Matthew 9.14-17	Ps 69.1-13
T	24	Revelation 5.1-14	Ps 71.1-13
F	25w	Galatians 1.11-24	Ps 76
S	26	Revelation 7.9-17	Ps 71.14-24

[w=Conversion of Paul, Apostle]

Week beginning 27 January
3rd in Ordinary Time
The Guiding Light

S	27x	Matthew 4.12-23	Ps 27
M	28	Judges 6.11-24	Ps 15
T	29	Luke 1.67-79	Ps 16
W	30	Judges 7.12-22	Ps 18.1-16
T	31	Philippians 2.12-18	Ps 18.17-30
F	1	John 1.6-9	Ps 19
S	2y	Luke 2.22-32	Ps 24

[x=Holocaust Memorial Day; y=Presentation of Christ in the Temple, Candlemas]

Week beginning 3 February
4th in Ordinary Time
Hunger for God

S	3z	Matthew 5.1-12	Ps 23
M	4	Ruth 1.1-18	Ps 25
T	5	Ruth 2.1-16	Ps 28
W	6aa	Matthew 6.1-21	Ps 51
T	7	Luke 6.17-26	Ps 29
F	8	Isaiah 65.1-16	Ps 31.1-18
S	9	Isaiah 65.17-25	Ps 31.19-24

[z=Education Sunday; aa=Ash Wednesday]

Week beginning 10 February
1st in Lent
Temptation and Forgiveness

S	10	Matthew 4.1-11	Ps 32
M	11	Genesis 4.1-16	Ps 38
T	12	Exodus 34.1-28	Ps 130
W	13	Matthew 18.6-14	Ps 34
T	14	1 Kings 19.1-8	Ps 36
F	15	Hebrews 4.14-5.14	Ps 51
S	16	Isaiah 58.1-12	Ps 39.1-13

Week beginning 17 February
2nd in Lent
Mission to the World

S	17	John 3.1-17	Ps 121
M	18	Isaiah 65.17-25	Ps 61
T	19	Ezekiel 36.22-32	Ps 62
W	20	John 8.1-11	Ps 63
T	21	Numbers 21.4-9	Ps 128
F	22	Romans 4.6-13	Ps 66
S	23	Colossians 1.15-23	Ps 67

Week beginning 24 February
3rd in Lent
Living Water

S	24	John 4.5-42	Ps 95
M	25	Genesis 24.1-27	Ps 1
T	26	Genesis 29.1-14	Ps 15
W	27	John 7.14-31, 37-39	Ps 77
T	28	Jeremiah 2.4-13	Ps 30
F	29	2 John 1-13	Ps 4
S	1	Exodus 17.1-7	Ps 6

Week beginning 2 March
4th in Lent
The Light of Christ

S	2ab	John 9.1-41	Ps 10
M	3	Isaiah 59.9-19	Ps 11
T	4	Isaiah 42.14-21	Ps 13
W	5	Matthew 9.27-34	Ps 14
T	6	Isaiah 60.17-22	Ps 15
F	ac	Acts 9.1-20	Ps 16
S	8	Numbers 9.15-23	Ps 18.1-16

[ab=Mothering Sunday;
ac=World Day of Prayer]

Week beginning 9 March
5th in Lent
Alive in Christ

S	9	John 11.1-45	Ps 18.47-51
M	10	1 Kings 17.17-24	Ps 19
T	11	2 Kings 4.18-37	Ps 143
W	12	Matthew 22.23-33	Ps 20
T	13	Jeremiah 32. 1-9, 36-41	Ps 21.1-7
F	14	Ephesians 2.1-10	Ps 25
S	15	1 Corinthians 15.12-22	Ps 27

Week beginning 16 March
Holy Week
Christ's Passion and Death

S	16ad	Matthew 26.14-27	Ps 24
M	17	John 12.1-11	Ps 71
T	18	John 12.20-36	Ps 28
W	19	John 13.21-32	Ps 31
T	20ae	1 Corinthians 11.23-26	Ps 23
F	21af	Hebrews 10.16-25	Ps 22
S	22ag	Job 14.1-14	Ps 36

[ad=Palm Sunday; ae=Maundy Thursday;
af=Good Friday; ag=Holy Saturday]

Week beginning 23 March
Easter Week
The Lord's Victory

S	23ah	John 20.1-18	Ps 118
M	24	Exodus 14.10-31	Ps 114
T	25	Exodus 15.20-21	Ps 111
W	26	Joshua 3.1-17	Ps 16
T	27	Matthew 28.1-10	Ps 116, 117
F	28	Colossians 3.1-17	Ps 121
S	29	Exodus 15.1-8	Ps 103

[ah=Easter Day]

Week beginning 30 March
2nd of Easter
God's Deliverance

S	30	John 20.19-31	Ps 37.1-16
M	31ai	Jonah 1.1-7	Ps 37.17-30
T	1aj	Matthew 12.38-42	Ps 37.31-41
W	2	Judges 6.36-40	Ps 48
T	3	1 Corinthians 15.12-28	Ps 54
F	4	Isaiah 25.6-9	Ps 113
S	5	Colossians 3.1-4	Ps 128

[ai=Annunciation of the Lord –trans;
aj =Joseph of Nazareth –trans]

Week beginning 6 April
3rd of Easter
The Lord's Feast

S	6	Luke 24.13-35	Ps 116
M	7	Genesis 18.1-4	Ps 56
T	8	Exodus 24.1-11	Ps 133
W	9	John 21.1-14	Ps 135
T	10	Proverbs 8.32-9.6	Ps 136
F	11	1 Peter 1.8-16	Ps 145
S	12	Revelation 3.14-22	Ps 146

Week beginning 13 April
4th of Easter
Shepherding of the Flock

S	13	John 10.1-10	Ps 23
M	14	Ezekiel 34.1-16	Ps 80
T	15	Ezekiel 34.23-31	Ps 110, 111
W	16	Matthew 20.17-28	Ps 112
T	17	Jeremiah 23.1-8	Ps 116, 117
F	18	1 Peter 2.9-17	Ps 130, 131
S	19	Revelation 7.13-17	Ps 132

Week beginning 20 April
5th of Easter
The Way, the Truth and the Life

S	20	John 14.1-14	Ps 147
M	21	Exodus 13.17-22	Ps 148
T	22	Proverbs 3.5-18	Ps 150
W	23	John 8.31-38	Ps 31
T	24	Isaiah 11.1-9	Ps 15
F	25ak	2 Timothy 4.1-11	Ps 45
S	26	Ezekiel 16.59-63	Ps 104

[ak=Mark, Evangelist]

Week beginning 27 April
6th of Easter
God's Promises

S	27	John 14.15-21	Ps 66
M	28	Deuteronomy 5.22-33	Ps 102
T	29	Deuteronomy 31.1-13	Ps 93
W	30	Acts 17.32-18.11	Ps 65
T	1al	Acts 1.1-11	Ps 47
F	2am	John 8.21-30	Ps 24
S	3	Ephesians 1.15-23	Ps 48

[al=Ascension Day;
am=Philip & James, Apostles-trans.]

Week beginning 4 May
1st after Ascension
Priestly Prayer

S	4	John 17.1-11	Ps 68
M	5	Leviticus 9.1-24	Ps 8
T	6	1 Kings 8.54-65	Ps 21
W	7	John 3.31-36	Ps 110, 111
T	8	Numbers 16.41-50	Ps 99, 100
F	9	1 Peter 3.21-4.11	Ps 20
S	10	Hebrews 10.19-25	Ps 68

Week beginning 11 May
Pentecost
Life in the Spirit

S	11an	John 20.19-23	Ps 104
M	12ao	Joel 2.18-29	Ps 48
T	13	Ezekiel 39.7-29	Ps 145.1-7
W	14ap	Acts 1.15-26	Ps 15
T	15	John 7.37-39	Ps 145.8-21
F	16	Numbers 11.24-30	Ps 46
S	17	Romans 8.14-27	Ps 150

[an=Pentecost; ao=Christian Aid Week;
ap=Matthias, Apostle]

Week beginning 18 May
Trinity
Joy in the Trinity

S	18aq	Matthew 28.16-20	Ps 8
M	19	Job 38.1-21	Ps 29
T	20	John 14.15-31	Ps 93
W	21	1 Kings 8.10-30	Ps 33
T	22	1 Corinthians 12.1-13	Ps 115
F	23	John 3.1-8	Ps 149
S	24ar	Romans 5.1-11	Ps 130

[aq=Trinity Sunday;
ar=Conversion of John Wesley]

Week beginning 25 May
8th in Ordinary Time
The Compassion of God

S	25	Matthew 6.24-34	Ps 103
M	26	Isaiah 49.8-16a	Ps 131
T	27	Hosea 11.1-12	Ps 66
W	28	Micah 7.18-20	Ps 71.1-13
T	29	Isaiah 52.7-10	Ps 80
F	30	Revelation 21.1-6	Ps 67
S	31	Revelation 22.1-5	Ps 139

Week beginning 1 June
9th in Ordinary Time
The Way of Wisdom
S 1 Matthew 7.21-29 Ps 46
M 2 Joshua 8.30-35 Ps 52
T 3 Joshua 24.1-28 Ps 56
W 4 Matthew 7.13-20 Ps 61
T 5 Job 28.12-28 Ps 63
F 6 Romans 3.9-22a Ps 69
S 7 Philippians 4.4-9 Ps 90

Week beginning 8 June
10th in Ordinary Time
The Everlasting Mercy
S 8 Matthew 9.9-13, 18-26 Ps 50
M 9 Hosea 8.11-14;
          10.1-2 Ps 71.1-14
T 10 Hosea 14.1-9 Ps 71.15-24
W11as Acts 14.18-20 Ps 19
T 12 Matthew 12.1-8 Ps 33
F 13 Hebrews 13.1-16 Ps 51
S 14 Ephesians 1.3-14 Ps 40
[World Refugee Week; as=Barnabas, Apostle]

Week beginning 15 June
11th in Ordinary Time
A Chosen People
S 15 Matthew 9.35-10.23 Ps 100
M 16 Joshua 1.1-11 Ps 116
T 17 1 Samuel 3.1-19 Ps 12
W 18 Luke 6.12-19 Ps 15
T 19 Proverbs 4.10-27 Ps 20
F 20 2 Thessalonians
          2.13-3.5 Ps 105
S 21 1 Peter 2.4-10 Ps 24

Week beginning 22 June
12th in Ordinary Time
The Cost of Discipleship
S 22 Matthew 10.24-39 Ps 69
M 23 Jeremiah 26.1-12 Ps 25
T 24at Luke 3.1-17 Ps 50
W 25 Jeremiah 38.1-13 Ps 26
T 26 Matthew 10.5-23 Ps 29
F 27 Micah 7.1-7 Ps 86
S 28 Revelation 2.1-11 Ps 6
[at=John the Baptist]

Week beginning 29 June
13th in Ordinary Time
Kingdom Demands
S 29 Matthew 10.40-42 Ps 13
M30au Acts 3.1-10 Ps 124
T 1 1 Kings 21.1-16 Ps 47
W 2 1 Kings 21.17-29 Ps 48
T 3av John 11.1-16 Ps 92
F 4 Matthew 11.16-24 Ps 54
S 5 1 John 4.1-6 Ps 72
[au=Peter, Apostle-trans;
av=Thomas, Apostle]

Week beginning 6 July
14th in Ordinary Time
The Yoke of Obedience
S 6 Matthew 11.16-19,
          25-30 Ps 45
M 7 Jeremiah 27.1-22 Ps 145
T 8 John 13.1-17 Ps 131
W 9 Jeremiah 13.1-11 Ps 75
T 10 Romans 7.1-20 Ps 76
F 11 Mark 8.31-33 Ps 80
S 12 Mark 8.34-38 Ps 142

Week beginning 13 July
15th in Ordinary Time
Parables of the Kingdom
S13aw Matthew 13.1-23 Ps 65
M 14 Matthew 13.24-30 Ps 66
T 15 Matthew 24.45-51 Ps 46
W 16 Luke 14.7-11 Ps 110, 111
T 17 Mark 4.26-29 Ps 121
F 18 Luke 16.1-8 Ps 124, 125
S 19 Luke 17.7-10 Ps 126, 127
[aw=NCH Sunday]

Week beginning 20 July
16th in Ordinary Time
The Final Ingathering
S 20 Matthew 24.36-43 Ps 132
M 21 Matthew 25.31-46 Ps 133
T 22ax Luke 8.1-3 Ps 42
W 23 Revelation 14.12-20 Ps 86
T 24 Daniel 12.1-13 Ps 118
F 25ay Mark 10.35-45 Ps 29
S 26 Nahum 1.1-13 Ps 139
[ax=Mary Magdalene; ay=James, Apostle]

Week beginning 27 July
17th in Ordinary Time
Wisdom and Understanding

S	27	Matthew 13.31-52	Ps 105.1-22
M	28	1 Kings 3.16-28	Ps 128
T	29	1 Kings 4.29-34	Ps 119.1-8
W	30	Mark 4.30-34	Ps 119.9-16
T	31	Proverbs 1.1-7, 20-23	Ps 119.17-24
F	1	Ephesians 6.10-18	Ps 119.25-32
S	2	John 1.1-14	Ps 119.33-40

Week beginning 3 August
18th in Ordinary Time
Bread of Heaven

S	3	Matthew 14.13-21	Ps 119.41-48
M	4	Deuteronomy 8.1-10	Ps 119.49-56
T	5	Deuteronomy 26.1-15	Ps 119.57-64
W	6az	1 John 3.1-3	Ps 27
T	7	Exodus 16.2-35	Ps 119.65-72
F	8	Acts 2.37-47	Ps 119.73-80
S	9	Luke 22.14-23	Ps 119.81-88

[az=The Transfiguration of the Lord]

Week beginning 10 August
19th in Ordinary Time
The Waters of Salvation

S	10	Matthew 14.22-33	Ps 119.89-96
M	11	Genesis 7.11-8.5	Ps 119.97-104
T	12	Matthew 8.23-27	Ps 119.105-112
W	13	Job 36.24-33	Ps 119.113-120
T	14	Job 37.14-24	Ps 119.121-128
F	15	Romans 6.3-8	Ps 119.129-136
S	16	Exodus 14.21-30	Ps 119.137-144

Week beginning 17 August
20th in Ordinary Time
A Healing God

S	17	Matthew 15.21-28	Ps 119.145-152
M	18	2 Kings 5.1-14	Ps 119.153-160
T	19	Isaiah 66.18-23	Ps 119.161-168
W	20	Matthew 8.1-13	Ps 119.169-176
T	21	Acts 3.1-10	Ps 67
F	22	Acts 19.11-20	Ps 133
S	23	Acts 28.1-6	Ps 121

Week beginning 24 August
21st in Ordinary Time
Rock-like Faith

S	24	Matthew 16.13-20	Ps 46
M	25ba	Luke 22.24-30	Ps 145
T	26	1 Samuel 7.3-13	Ps 55.1-8
W	27	Deuteronomy 32.18-39	Ps 55.16-22
T	28	Isaiah 28.14-22	Ps 18
F	29bb	Luke 3.1-20	Ps 146
S	30	Romans 9.30-10.4	Ps 124

[ba=Bartholemew, Apostle;
bb=The Beheading of John the Baptist]

Week beginning 31 August
22nd in Ordinary Time
Rebuking God's Servants

S	31	Matthew 16.21-28	Ps 105.1-26
M	1	Revelation 4.1-11	Ps 150
T	2	2 Samuel 11.27-12.15	Ps 51
W	3	Jeremiah 17.5-18	Ps 17
T	4	Acts 5.1-11	Ps 26
F	5	Galatians 3.1-14	Ps 130
S	6	Revelation 3.14-22	Ps 125

Thursday

Laudato si', mi' Signore, per frate Vento
et per aere et nubilo et sereno et onne tempo,
per lo quale, a le Tue creature dài sustentamento.

Yours be the praise, my Lord, for brother wind, for the atmosphere and clouds, and for our climate by which you sustain all life on earth.

Friday

Laudato si', mi Signore, per sor'Acqua.
la quale è multo utile et humile et pretiosa et casta.

Yours be the praise, my Lord, for sister water, who is so useful, humble, precious and pure.

Saturday

Laudato si', mi Signore, per frate Focu,
per lo quale ennallumini la nocte:
ed ello è bello et iocundo et robustoso et forte.

Yours be the praise, my Lord, for brother fire, who illumines the night, is ruddy and jolly and fierce and strong.

Sunday

Laudato si', mi Signore, per sora nostra matre Terra,
la quale ne sustenta et governa,
et produce diversi fructi con coloriti fior et herba.

Yours be the praise, my Lord, for mother Earth who supports and guides us and produces a rainbow of fruits and flowers and plants.

Laudate et benedicete mi Signore et rengratiate
e serviateli cum grande humilitate. Amen.

Praise and bless my Lord and humbly thank him and serve him. Amen.

Images: Monday, Thursday © Digital Vision, Tuesday, Wednesday, Friday, Saturday, Sunday © PureStockX

Day 15

Praying with Christians in the Middle East

O Good Shepherd, when the pastures are green let us share our fortune. When we walk through the shadows let us be comforted by your presence. When our cup overflows let us bring happiness to others. When we come to your house let us rejoice with the redeemed for ever. Amen.

John Hunter, 1849-1917

Israel/Palestine

Ecumenical Accompaniment Programme in Palestine and Israel (EAPPI):
December Departure:
Elizabeth Burroughs

Jordan

Lebanon

Almighty God,
your Word brought life and order upon the whole of creation, and your Word is still creating life today.
To you everything is uniquely valuable.
To you everyone is equally special.
   Forgive us that we do not value human life sufficiently,
   that we allow our fellow human beings to be
   persecuted, abused, damaged and destroyed.
We pray for the troubled lands of **Israel**, **Palestine** and the **Lebanon**, the place that we like to call the Holy Land.
We pray for the persecuted –
   and for those who persecute them;
for the abused – and for those who abuse them;
for the damaged – and for those who damage them;
for those whose dignity is destroyed –
   and for those who destroy it.
   And we pray for the peacemakers that they may begin
   to build bridges of understanding to replace the barriers
   of distrust.
We pray in the name of Jesus Christ, the Lord of hope and the bringer of peace. Amen.

Elizabeth Burroughs, Ecumenical Accompanier 2006

Bill Anderson

Light a candle for peace
With a candle of hope burning, one light dispelling all darkness, we pray, Lord, that you may grant peace to the land we call Holy.
Help us to see beyond politics to people, the living stones.
We pray for the work of:
the Bethlehem Arab Society for Rehabilitation in Beit Jala, Bethlehem and its Director, Edmund Shehadeh;
the Evangelical School in Ramallah;
the Ahli Arab Hospital in Gaza City;
the Holyland Institute for the Deaf in Salt, **Jordan**;
all 13 Church leaders in Jerusalem from both Western and Eastern traditions, that they may continue their ecumenical partnership united in declaring the gospel of peace and reconciliation.

Alan Ashton, retired Minister, Cambridge

We pray for the Isle of Man District as ways are sought to organize the District most effectively;
for the District to continue to find ways of being truly relevant in the present age while keeping faith with our traditions and history.
We pray that we may become a light of challenge and a light of guidance, with the presence of Christ being seen as a living reality.

**Isle of Man District
Rheynn Ellan Vannin Yn Agglish Haasilagh**
Chair:
Malcolm Peacock

Malcolm Peacock

Embracing clouds,
whispering winds,
singing seas,
remind us of the presence of God.
We give thanks for creative love.

History engraved on landscape,
landscape embraced by buildings,
remind us of the present God.
We give thanks for sustaining love.

Headlights moving in the dark,
trails of roads,
engines racing,
remind us of the persistent God.
We give thanks for transforming love.

Banner headlines,
footsore politicians,
strident voices,
remind us of the pertinent God.
We give thanks for restoring love.

In beauty,
history,
challenge
and change
we are held by the love of God
who would make us and all things new.
Amen.

Malcolm Peacock, Isle of Man District Chair

God, your love embraces all
and all are welcome to partake of your feast,
the gospel feast of your words and wisdom,
the sacrificial feast of your body and soul. Amen.

Hyacinth Sweeney, creative writer

He built the earth, he spread the sky and fixed the starry lights on high.
H&P 22

Day 16

Praying with Christians in the Indian Subcontinent

Lord Jesus Christ, Wisdom and Word of God, dwell in our hearts, by your most Holy Spirit, that out of the abundance of our hearts our mouths may speak your praise. Amen.

Christina Rossetti, 1830-94

Church of Bangladesh

Moderator:
Michael Baroi

Mission Partners:
t/ed David and Sarah Hall,
    Rebecca and Reuben
sd James Pender
d Helen Brannam
(all joint appointments
    with CofS, CMS, USPG
    and CWM)

Scholarship student:
Heman Halder°
    (in Singapore)

Church of Pakistan

Moderator:
Alexander Malik

Dear Lord, the roots of the mango trees,
exposed to the wind are binding the soil.
A thousand mango trees stand in silent witness
to the cost of independence
in the face of an alien wind.
    Gnarled in the face of drought;
    there's no monsoon rain
    to freshen the leaves.
    The fruit is small, though still sweet.
May the mango roots dig deep,
holding the soil of our deepest desires,
never to be cut, while we live in peace.
    May justice blossom again
    and wisdom be found like sap.
    While demands increase upon the land,
    may steadfast love hold us like limbs
    as we work from among the people.
And may there always be rice, dahl and
a little mango fruit, to welcome our
neighbours, when the rains come. Amen.

John Bennett, former Mission Partner, Bangladesh

We pray for the security of **Pakistan** and the strengthening of the delicate peace that exists.
Give thanks that the Church of Pakistan is able to work creatively within society through many programmes and institutions enabling the Christian message to be heard.
We pray for the work of Church World Service Pakistan/ Afghanistan that has been supporting oppressed communities by engaging in development and relief initiatives, poverty reduction, women's empowerment, building communal harmony and peace, advocacy on socio-political issues and strengthening civil society organizations.

Belfast District

Superintendent:
W. Brian Fletcher

Belfast's Titanic Quarter

We give thanks to God for new possibilities in mission; and for the fresh spiritual life that many churches in Belfast are experiencing through the 24/7 prayer movement. We pray for everyone involved in education as falling numbers in many schools mean closures and uncertainty; for the District Secretary, Derek Johnston; for plans to establish a Christian presence and witness in the new 'Titanic Quarter' development.

Gracious Father, God of truth and grace, save us from falsehood in our thinking, our speaking and our living, and grant that your grace may so flood our lives that it overflows to bless the lives of all whom we meet, for the glory of your name. Amen.

Donald Ker, Secretary of the Irish Methodist Church Conference

Leeds District

Chair:
Liz Smith

Give thanks for the increasing willingness of churches and circuits to take risks in exploring new ventures in mission. We pray for the District as it receives a new Chair, six new Superintendents and four Probationers, that new ministries may encourage new ways forward; for the Nigeria Health Care Project whose Chair, Peter Grubb, and Vice-Chair, Margaret Webb, are members at Christ Church, Halton, and have been made Knights of John Wesley by the Methodist Church of Nigeria; for Bev Hollings, the Evangelism Enabler.

God, whose love embraces all
and whose patience with us never comes to an end,
form us after the pattern of Christ, that we may have
tongues to speak and sing your good news,
hearts to love you and our neighbours,
and lives which embody the values of your reign. Amen.

Michael Townsend, Leeds District

Lord of all quiet thoughts and prayers, be my guide. Because you were lowly, I will adore you; because you came as a servant, command me and I will serve you; because your yoke is easy, I will labour for you with all my strength. Help me to see in others, however mean, the image of yourself and bring me, at last, to eternal life, through Jesus Christ my Lord. Amen.

Selwyn Veater, Prayer Co-ordinator, Brighton and Hove Circuit

Inscribed upon the cross we see in shining letters, 'God is love'.

H&P 182

49

Day 17

Praying with Christians in India

O God, the Sun behind all suns and the Being behind all being, draw near to us in every friend we possess and in every enemy who crosses our path. Let us see your glory in the greyness of the dawn, in the eye of the storm and in the trivial sacraments of everyday life; through Christ our Lord. Amen.

George Macleod, 1895-1991

Church of North India (CNI)

Moderator:
Joel V. Mal

Scholarship Student:
Anugrah Ramble°
(in Britain)

Church of South India (CSI)

Moderator:
Peter Sugandhar

Experience Exchange:
George and Mione
Goldspink
Thomas Jones

Scholarship Student:
George Cornelius
Tantepudi°
(in Singapore)

We pray for **India** with its vast and growing population, its many cultures, many faiths and many different languages; for the Women's Hostel in Passumalai, in Madurai, Tamil Nadu, South India, which provides a safe refuge for battered, abused and abandoned women and their children. We pray that they may find the staff they need to continue their life-saving work; for the Hospice at Bangapuram, Tamil Nadu, South India, where adults and children with HIV/AIDS are treated and cared for;

that your healing love may bring peace of mind to all who are burdened by guilt, fear or rejection as a result of their condition;

for the lovely children born with a devastating heritage which will deny them many future opportunities.

Mary Eden, former EEP

O God! We have cried for you; hear us, O Lord.
We see the world's beauty, your beautiful work of art;
we have failed to preserve it.
We see war, the loss of life and property;
we have failed to establish your love.
We see hatred and enmity;
we have failed to make friends.
We see corruption due to selfish motives;
we have failed to build a just community.
We see people starving;
we have failed to provide them with food.
We see people homeless;
we have failed to provide them with shelter.
It is always we who have failed, you never.
You have truly blessed us; we have destroyed your blessings.
Give us wisdom to restore nature and its beauty,
that we may love and care for this beautiful gift.
Teach us and guide us to be obedient and faithful in this life.
Hold our hands until the last breath,
so that we can remain with you forever. Amen.

Ajay Singh, Minster, Swindon & Marlborough Circuit
from the Diocese of Lucknow, CNI, Allahabad, India

We give thanks for all the faithful loving and caring which underpins the life of our churches.

We pray for the inspiration and encouragement of the Holy Spirit as we continue to reshape our common life for mission; for the Synod Secretary, Mike Childs.

Lincoln and Grimsby District

Chair:
David Perry

Migrant workers' prayer
Our God, parent of all living beings,
help us to open our hearts and minds
to the needs of others,
especially the strangers living here among us:
the women, men and children from Portugal, Poland,
Lithuania, Latvia and many other countries.
Let us share your bounteous grace with them:
there is enough food and work for everybody.
Let us help them to realize their aspirations for
a better life
in peace and freedom for themselves,
their families and us.
Let us show them the respect they deserve
as your children
and help us to protect them from the evils
of racism and exploitation.
Help us to see you in them. Amen.

David de Verny, Migrant Workers' Chaplain,
Lincolnshire Chaplaincy Services

Dancers (Shine Photographics and Media)

Loving God, we thank you
for your love and care that spans the generations.
for your Holy Spirit who enfolds us and strengthens us.
Help us to be faithful disciples.

We pray for those who are struggling to pray.
We intercede for those who are yearning
for your peace and protection.
We pray for actions that speak louder than words.

May we see the image of the invisible God
in the worship and service that we share with others.
Confront us with the passion, innovation and energy
that is transforming the work of the Church,
so that wherever we find ourselves, we will be encouraged.
Amen.

Langley Mackrell-Hey, Lincoln South Circuit
and Director, Shine Photographics and Media

The earth
so bright,
so full of
splendour
and joy.

H&P 564

51

Day 18

Praying with Christians in Asia

Lord, as you have taught us the folly of gaining the whole world and losing ourselves, grant us grace so to lose ourselves that we may find ourselves made new, and so to forget ourselves that we may be remembered in your kingdom; through Christ our Lord. Amen.

Reinhold Niebuhr, 1892-1971

Myanmar/Burma
The Methodist Church of Upper Myanmar

Methodist President:
C. Kapa

Scholarship students:
Ngurliana° (in Britain)
San Pwint
(in Philippines)
Lan Din Puii° (in Malaysia)
Mya Sanda (in Japan)
Kok Thang° (Malaysia)
Khawsiama° (Khin Muang Yee) (in Hong Kong)
C. Kapa° (in Myanmar)

Nepal
The United Mission to Nepal (UMN)

Director of the UMN:
Jennie Collins

Mission Partners:
ad/p Paul and Sarah Wright,
Jack and Asha
ad/ad Michael and Maureen Hawksworth
t/ed Allan and Andrea Smith

Scholarship students:
Susan Rai (in Nepal)
Bibhu Singh (in Nepal)

Come, God Almighty, make us truly your own.
May our desires be truly your desires;
may our hopes be truly your hopes;
may our wills be truly in step with your will;
may all our days be your days, O Lord.
For you are our only strength and support.
Come close, O Lord, and dwell with us. Amen.

*Allan and Andrea Smith, Mission Partners in **Nepal***

God of life and truth,
    let us be wary of easy and superficial responses;
    help us find the depths of our souls.
God of justice and peace,
    let us be angry at oppression and exploitation;
    help us to use inner resources to combat injustice.
God of comfort and joy,
    let us cry out against war, pain, rejection, starvation;
    help us with understanding and empathy,
so that we can believe that we can make a difference
    in the world
through you, and in your name.
And let us be fools for Christ. Amen.

Christine Elliott, World Church Secretary, Asia Pacific

Jesus,
you turned over the traders' tables,
kicked up a fuss,
shouted and screamed,
suffered and died,
challenged injustice.
We repent of the times when we
have kept our heads down,
have shut our mouths,
have played it safe,
ignored injustice.

Forgive us and breathe your Spirit into us, we pray. Amen.

Sarah Hagger, MRDF

Deb Bahadur Rana producing honey from new beehives with help from MRDF partners in Nepal (© MRDF/Kirsty Smith)

Liverpool District

Chair:
James Booth

Mission Partners:
Marcus° and Sylvia Torchon and Jean-de-Luc René (MCCA)

We give thanks for all those people God has given who live, work, worship and witness in the Liverpool District; for the ministry of the mission partner Revd Marcus Torchon. We pray for the city of Liverpool as it becomes the European Capital of Culture in 2008, that the opportunities for regeneration that this presents will be seized, serving the whole community and region; for our working ecumenically that, together with other churches, we may develop effective ministry and mission across the region using all the resources that God has given us; for the work of the Synod Secretary, Phillipa Sudlow, and mission partners working in the Liverpool District.

Living Lord,
open our eyes to the reality of your world as it is, in its need of you;
open our eyes to the reality of our lives as we are, in our need of you;
open our eyes to the reality of your love for the whole of your creation;
open my eyes to the reality of your love for me;
open our eyes to Jesus.
Visit us with your salvation – and may we play our part, day by day, in its coming.
Through Jesus Christ, our Lord and Saviour. Amen.

James Booth, Liverpool District Chair

God, creator of this world, one yet divided, forgive us that we allow divisions between ourselves and people of other faiths and so add to instability in the world.
Teach us that it is the responsibility of us all to reach out with the hands of friendship and build safer communities.
Help us, God of all, to work for peace. Amen.

Gary Hopkins, Methodist Youth Executive

God's words
Lord Jesus Christ, we offer you thanks for your life-giving words to us. We ask that you send your Holy Spirit into our hearts and minds as we welcome your influence there.
We acknowledge that you live in the changing seasons, in their continuous dying and living again.
We believe that you live in every heart which loves you and that everything has its beginning and fulfils its purpose in you. We worship you, the reality behind everything and rejoice that your name is Love. Amen.

Jenny Wakelin, Local Preacher, St Albans & Welwyn Circuit

Bring us eyes thy book to read.
H&P 468

53

Day 19

Praying with Christians in Asia

Lord, may the doors of our homes be wide enough to receive those in need; and narrow enough to shut out all envy and pride. May each threshold be smooth enough to provide no stumbling block to children or straying feet. Let the entrance be rugged and strong enough to turn back the tempter's power. May those who enter find the gateway to your eternal kingdom. Amen.

Thomas Ken, 1637-1711

Sri Lanka
Methodist President:
Ebeneezer Joseph

Mission Partners:
th/ad Rosemary Fletcher°
    and James Rowley
lib Margaret (née Julian)
    and Kithiri Mudalige
    and Nathan (+USPG)

Scholarship Students:
M.G. Edmund° (in Britain)
th/th Chellian° and
    Malar° Lawrence, Felix
    and Felicita

Indonesia and East Timor
Gereja Methodist Bishop:
H. Doloksaribu

Collect from the Theological College of Lanka
Gracious God, we humbly pray with your mercy and favour to behold the Theological College of Lanka, especially its Principal, the Revd Dr Albert W. Jebanesan, and all the staff and students, that knowledge may increase and abound. Bless all who teach and all who learn, and grant that in humility we may ever look to you, who is the fountain of all wisdom. We pray in the name of the Triune God, who is community. Amen.

Loving Father, we come to you with our hearts burdened for the island of **Sri Lanka**, beset by ethnic conflict, political and religious tensions, social and economic problems. Thank you for the courage with which you strengthen your people who live and work in situations that many of us simply cannot comprehend. As your love impels them to reach out to those in their communities who are suffering physically and emotionally, to those traumatized by ethnic conflict, both civilian and soldier, may your people reflect your beauty, love, grace and forgiveness as they live out the Word of life, as they speak words of life and hope into the darkness that has invaded so many lives, and as they stoop to raise people up. Amen.

Maggie Mudalige, Librarian, Theological College of Lanka, Sri Lanka

Gracious and loving Father, who created all things, we beseech you to forgive us for our disobedience, which has caused your good creation to turn into evil and has ruined its beauty and equity. You made men and women equal, without the horror of poverty. But we, through selfishness and avarice, have caused disparities to enter the perfect world system that you created. Amen.

Leo Fonseka, MRDF Partner, Methodist Church in Sri Lanka

We pray for the different communities within the Methodist Church in **Indonesia**. May they have wisdom and compassion in their difference. We remember all those who have been affected by natural disasters in recent times as they rebuild their lives. Amen.

Manchester and Stockport District

Chair:
Keith Davies

We give thanks for all the signs of new life in the Manchester and Stockport District;
for churches and circuits prepared to take risks in mission;
for new work with children and young people across the District;
for the growing number of fresh expressions of church;
for the faithful witness of Methodist communities, not least in the most deprived areas.
We pray for the newly formed Regional Training Partnership and its Director, Anne Dawtry;
for Fred Bell, the Synod Secretary;
for Pete Shepherd, the new District Mission Enabler;
for Rosemary Kidd, the Training and Development Officer;
for Graham Kent, the Ecumenical Development Officer for Greater Manchester Churches Together;
for the many District officers who support and facilitate God's work and mission within the District.

God of life and love, we turn to you and you welcome us;
you invite us to follow you and to learn the ways of your Son.
Thank you for the perfect forgiveness we find in you.
You are our stillness and our strength;
you are our peace and our joy.
By your grace, mould us according to your desires,
that we may be shaped by the purposes of your kingdom.
Help us to celebrate your unique expression
in each person we meet.
May your love overwhelm us;
may your gentleness refresh us;
may your passion inspire us. Amen.

Keith Davies, Manchester and Stockport District Chair

Creator God,
today you took back the life you gave so fleetingly,
sleeping peacefully now in your arms instead of ours.
We ask your loving hand to care for
this child, and for all who have gone.
Hug them for us, for they are beyond our reach for
a short while.
And for the loving ones left behind,
give them the courage to trust, to hope, to smile again,
to know that their child is safe with you. Amen.

Jacqui Hicks, Chislehurst

Soon shall every tear be dry.

H&P 717

55

Day 20

Praying with Christians in Asia

Each day and each night, may the wisdom of the Wonderful Counsellor guide us. May the strength of the Mighty God defend us. May the love of the Everlasting Father enfold us and may the blessing of the Prince of Peace rest upon us; now and always. Amen.

Based on Isaiah of Jerusalem (8th century BC)

Singapore

Methodist Bishop:
Robert Solomon

Mission Partners:
ed John° and Sally Barratt
th/ed Steven° and Lorraine Emery-Wright and Hannah

Malaysia

Methodist Bishop:
Hwa Yung

Mission Partners:
th David and Rhona Burfield

Scholarship Student:
Anthony Loke (in Britain)

Heavenly Father, we thank and praise you for your love and protection for the nation of **Singapore**; for the peace and abundance and the harmony among people of various races and faiths. We pray that you will continue to watch over the Methodist Church in Singapore, and unite us as we come together as one body to serve you and our community. We offer this prayer in Jesus' most holy name. Amen.

Peter Teo, Editor, Methodist Message, Singapore

Dear God of all creation, you make all things bright and beautiful. You blend the flowers so intricately in their awesome and wonderful colours. You speak, and the animals come to life, crawling, creeping, hopping, running and walking, each in their unique way. You make the moon, the stars and the sun for us to behold and to know that you are God, the source of all light. In these days of change and transition, you do not change. You are forever the same: yesterday, today and forever. Help me all through life, to focus on you and your purpose for me. Help me be the person you want me to be, all for your glory. Therefore, I offer myself to you, to be that shining light as a servant of Jesus. In his name, I pray. Amen.

David Wee, WCBP, Singapore/Hull

We pray for Christians in **Malaysia**, that they may give a clear witness to Christ in a multi-religious society where Islam is the majority religion;
that they may learn to live simply and give sacrificially in the midst of the pressure of materialism;
that they may work for social justice for all people regardless of race or religion;
that secondary school and college students living away from home may remain faithful to Jesus amidst challenges to their faith;
and that Bible colleges and seminaries may effectively train men and women to be skilled and godly pastors. Amen.

*David Burfield,
Mission Partner, Sabah Theological Seminary, Malaysia*

We give thanks for new, refurbished and extended buildings at Wrekenton, West Harton and Fence Houses and for the mission opportunities they present.

We pray for fresh expressions of church in our District and especially for the Ruth Project in Stanley, Cell Networks in Consett and Café Church in Jesmond;

for the work of Elizabeth Edwards, Synod Secretary, Revd Stephen Lindridge, Evangelism Enabler, Revd Andrew Letby, Regional Economic Mission Enabler and Mark Bagnall, Regional Training and Development Officer.

Newcastle upon Tyne District

Chair:
Leo Osborn

Lord Jesus Christ,
in you all things in heaven and on earth hold together.
In your love and mercy protect the helpless,
embrace the outcast,
carry the weak
and bring home the lost
so that we, with all creation, may be made one in you
and the whole earth live to praise your name
to the Father's glory. Amen.

Leo Osborn, Newcastle upon Tyne District Chair

Statue of St Aidan near Holy Island (Leo Osborn)

Give to us, O Lord,
the peace of those who have learned to serve you,
the peace of those who are glad to obey you,
and the peace of those who rejoice in your praise,
through Christ our Lord. Amen.

St Aidan

Laundry prayer

God, you have washed me clean and dried me,
now turn me upside down and shake me out.
Discharge the static when I cling to things,
smooth out the creases, brush away the fluff.
Pull me, reshape me, turn me right side out,
iron me and air me, ready to be used.
Let me not be afraid of dirt and sweat,
repair me if I split, patch up my wear,
but please, never leave me on the shelf,
outdated, out of fashion, past repair. Amen.

*© Diane Coleman, local preacher and
Warden of Norwood Day Retreat Centre*

Awake
my soul,
and sing!

H&P 255

57

Day 21

Praying with Christians in East Asia

Let our trust be in you, O God, that nothing may disturb us or frighten us. Teach us that all things are passing and that you are changeless. In patience let us strive and quietly achieve. You alone meet every need and in you we can lack nothing. Amen.

Teresa of Avila, 1515-82

China

President of China Christian Council:
Cao Shengjie

Amity Teachers:
David Clements
Angela Evans
Christine Green
Ian Groves
Katherine Jarman
Mick and Anne Kavanagh
Gordon Paterson
Kath Saltwell

Amity is a Chinese non-Government Organization founded by Christians

Hong Kong (Special Administrative Region of China)

Methodist President:
Lo Lung Kwong

Give thanks to God for the growing Church in **China**, for the many new believers who are coming to faith in Christ there and for the Christians in China who attract others through their passion and dedication to their faith.
Pray for pastors to guide this growing flock; for the Church in China to mature and grow, that it may be able to engage with those who will influence the future direction of this emerging superpower;
for God to open the hearts and minds of those who write and implement religious policy in China, that all believers may enjoy growing space to worship and practise their faith freely;
for the work of the Amity Foundation in printing Bibles and ministering to those in need within Chinese society.

Ian Groves, formerly seconded to the Hong Kong office of the Amity Foundation

We pray for wisdom and integrity for China's leaders as China meets the glare of world attention in the Olympic Games in 2008, environmental threats confront urban and rural communities and the glories of creation across a nation rich in diversity, and communities face the growing inequalities between the wealthy and poor. Amen.

Alison Lewis

China today:
a country, poised to display its modernity at the Olympic Games,
but deeply conscious of both its recent and its distant past;
a Communist government encouraging a capitalist economy
producing extraordinary wealth and widespread poverty;
an exclusive, Great Wall, mentality, yet
urgent to become a powerful player in the world;
ancient cities, enduring endless change,
as revered structures are swept away for the new;
a traditional people in a constant state of flux,
changing jobs, changing residencies,
travelling from villages to soulless megacities.
China today!

John Sampson, Friends of the Church in China

Thank you, God, for the District Celebration, 'Lost in wonder love and praise'. May we always live in the light of your steadfast love and plentiful mercies.

We pray that you will bless with courage, faithfulness and winsomeness all pastoral visitors and magazine distributors who knock on doors and by their prayers and love seek to make Christ famous.

Down District

Superintendent:
Kenneth Todd

Give thanks for churches and circuits taking bold and sometimes painful decisions about the future;

for the newly created Trinity church at Goosnargh;

for the opening of Wesley's café in Garstang,

for the vision of one new church to serve the community of Thornton in the Fleetwood circuit;

for exciting ecumenical developments in Great Harwood and their commitment to a new building.

Pray for Dale Barton, the Churches Together in Lancashire Inter-Faith Officer, and particularly for the Building Bridges project in Burnley, based in the Ibrahim mosque, which seeks to create good relationships between the faith communities;

for all the churches within the District as they seek, through the District's three-year priorities, to enable every member of the faith community to become the Living Presence of Christ in every aspect of their lives;

for the continuing prayer initiative which holds everything together.

North Lancashire District

Chair:
Stephen Poxon

Mission Partners:
Garoº and Dada Kilagi, Geua, Gima and Elijah (Papua New Guinea)

Caring, loving God,
you call us to journey with Jesus.
Help me to hear you calling me by name
as I seek to turn to you again.
Give me the courage to face life's temptations
and so discover a deeper faith in you.
Caring, loving God,
release your Spirit within me,
that I may become the living presence of Christ
wherever you may place me. Amen.

District Prayer for 'Being the Living Presence of Christ'

Hark, my soul! It is the Lord.

H&P 521

Day 22

Praying with Christians in East Asia

Lord God, in whom we live and move and have our being, open our eyes to your fatherly presence forever around us. Draw our hearts with the power of your love and teach us to be anxious for nothing. Take from us all doubt and mistrust and lift our thoughts heavenwards into the light of your glory; through Christ our Lord. Amen.

Brooke Foss Westcott, 1825-1901

Japan

General Secretary of the Kyodan, the United Church of Christ in Japan:
Noboru Takemae

Mission Partners:
ed Sheila Norris
ed Daniel and Yasuko
    Dellming, Momoko,
    Daisuke and Yoko

Korea

Presiding Bishop
Kwang Young

In **Japan**, a large number of men see little of their children due to the pressure of work. We pray for mothers who stay at home alone with their children – often without grandparents and relatives nearby – who are sometimes driven by stress to abuse their children. We pray that Christians will be loving neighbours to them and that the Church may be a place of quiet and rest for them.

Yasuko Dellming, Mission Partner, Japan

Give thanks for the witness of the Japanese Church where, at only about one per cent of the population, Christians are a small minority, and yet their influence has been far greater than their numbers would suggest, as they act as the 'salt of the earth'.
We pray for the Buraku Liberation Center, which focuses on the needs of some three million people of 'Buraku' descent who still face discrimination as a legacy of the caste-like system of feudal days.

Ueda Hiroko, Mission Secretary, UCCJ

Praise God! Christians from North and South **Korea**
gather as one, uniting in praise,
dispelling the weariness of long, dark years of division.
O God, we pray that we may become living witnesses of the resurrection. Let our hands, bloodied by hammering the nails of hatred and thrusting the spear of condemnation, become hands that bind the wounds and reach out in reconciliation. Let us regain our voices of comfort, our steps of peace, and let us finally realize that we can transform the history of death. May our incomplete liberation become perfect reunification. May the Easter greeting 'Peace be with you' reach beyond our land to Asia and to all the world and unite us all in peace, joyful shouts, laughter, the embrace of friendship. And may the uncertain days of the global village become, rather, the third day of hope, a new creation. Amen.

Adapted from a common Easter prayer by the National Council of Churches in Korea (South) and Korean Christian Federation (North)

Nottingham and Derby District

Chair:
Wesley Blakey

Give thanks for the people of God of this District who constantly give their time and energy to encourage one another and work to create a vision of what is possible in God's name.

Pray for the work of Helen Watson, the Synod Secretary; for chaplains in prisons; hospitals; industry, universities; schools and colleges and for the emergency services; for the South Derbyshire Circuit, as it seeks to reshape for modern mission, that the Swadlincote Partnership between social agencies and the church – where premises, workers and all other resources will be shared – will enable the gospel to be shared in a positive and realistic way.

Father God, in our everyday lives, with your guidance, may we turn ordinary days into special days as we look for new ways of serving you. And in our serving may our lives be enriched and our witness strengthened.
Cover us, with your everlasting arms of love when things seem difficult.
Help us to see you in a new way when the familiar seems distant.
Allow us to explore the variety of ways in which we can introduce you to others.
Never let us hold on to our way of doing things if it stops another from finding you.
Give us grace, to place ourselves completely in your care and guidance.
Everything we have is a gift from you, help us to use all that we have for your honour and glory. Amen.

Edward and Marjorie Adams, Newark and Southwell Circuit

May I always do the best I can and
    listen before judging
    think before speaking
    admit I may be wrong
    be prompt in keeping promises
    be generous to one who has hurt me
    ask pardon when in error
    put the best interpretation on the acts of others.
So that I may never go to sleep wishing things had been different. Amen.

Wesley Blakey

In the rush and noise of life, as you have intervals, step within yourself and be still. Wait upon God and feel his good presence; this will carry you through your day's business.

William Penn (1644-1718)

Christian, love me more.

H&P 141

Day 23

Praying with Christians in Australia and New Zealand

Gracious God, let the light of your face shine upon us. Let your peace rule in our hearts, your strength be our song and your grace be sufficient for our need. Prepare us for the events of each day that we may take up our cross and follow in the steps of our Lord and Saviour, Jesus Christ. Amen.

Matthew Henry, 1662-1714

Aotearoa/ New Zealand

Methodist President:
John Salmon

The Uniting Church of Australia (UCA)

President:
James Haire

We pray for the many children who are at risk from poverty and child abuse;
that high levels of violent behaviour may be reduced;
that we might address climate change issues now and with vigour;
for mutual respect in a society that is becoming increasingly diverse – both culturally and religiously;
that churches may work together to address these and other issues in their communities.

*John H. Roberts, Mission and Ecumenical Secretary, Methodist Church of **New Zealand***

Adrian Burdon

> God of the southern skies:
> we have been blessed with an abundance
>   of good things.
> Yet all is not well in the 'land of the long white cloud'*:
> there is an unjust distribution of wealth,
> people are suffering,
> minorities are sidelined,
> the land is hurting,
> churches remain divided.
> Bring all things together in the Spirit of Christ,
> that there may be fullness of life in Aotearoa
> for all people,
> for earth, sea and sky. Amen.
>
> *John Roberts*

We give thanks for the Young Ambassadors for Peace Programme in **Australia**. The programme offers positive approaches to finding lasting peaceful solutions in situations of conflict.
Pray for the workshop leaders and participants as each grow in their understanding of working with issues of power, discrimination, mediation, negotiation and peaceful resolution of conflict.

*Aotearoa, which means 'long white cloud', is the indigenous Māori name for New Zealand

Give thanks for exciting new growth and fresh expressions of being church within the District;
for the varied additional gifts for God's work, brought together through enlarging the District.
Pray for the Revd Tim Woolley as he takes on new responsibilities as District Director of Mission;
for his family as they settle within their new community;
for specialist deacons, lay people and those who enable the work of God in new communities within the District.

> All are welcome – yet we prefer those we know.
> All are invited – yet we always check credentials.
> All is ready – yet we find reason for delay.
> God of grace and mercy and compassion
> reignite our faith
> reinvigorate our courage
> and free us from fear,
> so that, rejoicing in your love,
> we may genuinely welcome all
> to the feast of your goodness and truth. Amen.
>
> *Alison Tomlin, Northampton District Chair*

Welcoming God, you invite all people to share in the feast of your love and mercy in Jesus Christ. We praise you for your gracious invitation which extends to both rich and poor, to the loved, the unloved and the unlovable. Your invitation reaches out to touch the lives of the privileged and the needy, the proud and the humble. We praise and worship you for your open invitation in Jesus Christ. Forgive us when we think 'all' means 'all those people like us'. Forgive our blinkered vision and our closed minds, and open our eyes and our hearts to the truth of your all-encompassing invitation in Jesus Christ. Amen.

Jan Grimwood, Local Preacher, Oxford Circuit

Lord God, parent and creator, present in all your creation, from the smallest atom to the highest mountain, help us to recognize you at work in our lives and in your creation around us.
Lord Jesus, you crossed the ultimate divide between heaven and earth, showing how much each one of us is loved, help us to accept your love and to share it with others.
Holy Spirit, encourager and guide in all we think, say and do, help us to remember to seek your help and guidance in our daily living.
All-embracing God, we give you thanks and praise. Amen.

Elaine Turner, Connexional Women's Network President 2004-5

Northampton District

Chair:
Alison Tomlin

Mission Partners:
Edward° and Esther Sakwe, Electa, Lucella, Masoma and Jemea (Cameroon)
Asif° and Rohama° Karam, Zarah, Zoya and Zeenia (Pakistan)

Fairford Leys Church, in the Northampton District (Paul Taylor)

All for Jesus – all for Jesus – this the Church's song must be.
H&P 251

Day 24

Praying with Christians in the Pacific

Lord, you have taught us that all our doings without love are worth nothing. Send your Holy Spirit, and pour into our hearts that most excellent of love, the bond of all peace and virtues, without which those who live are counted as dead before you. And this we ask for the sake of your Son, our Saviour Jesus Christ. Amen.

Thomas Cranmer, 1489-1556

United Church in Papua New Guinea

Moderator:
Samson Lowa
t/m John and Jenny
Willetts, Daniel and
Peter

We give thanks for the work of Bible Translators, Tim and Karen Schlatter, who, for the last 17 years have been working with the Tabo people in the Western Province of **Papua New Guinea** to complete translations of the New Testament in the two main Tabo dialects. We praise you, Lord, because, now that they have access to the Scriptures, many people in this region have turned to Christ. We pray for the work of 16 pastors and lay pastors ministering to the Tabo people in their own language.

United Church of the Solomon Islands

Moderator:
David Havea

ed/n Richard and Kathryn
Jackson
m/m Mark and Elizabeth
Leeming, Molly, Caleb
and Naomi

Lord, we thank you for the **Solomon Islands**, so blessed with natural beauty: flora, fauna, landscape and people, which truly express and reflect your perfect and unique creation. Lord, we pray for your wisdom upon the people and leaders in the Solomon Islands; families, tribal chiefs, church pastors, ministers, business people, politicians, young people, women and children. Lead these people to your wisdom, peace and righteousness. May they be comforted and strengthened by your word, love, unity and peace. May the ethnic and cultural differences within the Islands create a unique nation that upholds your kingdom values. Amen.

David Barakana Havea, Moderator,
United Church in the Solomon Islands

Scholarship Students:
Mose Fuaiva'a°
  (in Britain)

God, help us
to guard and shield the most vulnerable and the weak,
to work for justice and freedom,
that all may taste your love.
May we be
risk-takers
life-givers
courageous
in your mission. Amen.

Christine Elliott, World Church Secretary, Asia Pacific

Plymouth and Exeter District

Chair:
John Carne

Gracious God, we give thanks for new initiatives in the Plymouth and Exeter District that seek to celebrate and witness to the Gospel.

We give thanks for the District emphasis on partnership which has encouraged circuits to come together; we pray for the new circuits of Taunton Deane and South Sedgemoor, Ilfracombe and Barnstaple, and South Devon.

We give thanks for all ecumenical opportunities and we pray for growing relationships which seek to value the gifts that denominations can offer to each other.

We give thanks for fresh expressions of church being explored and worked with in the District, and pray that these will bring renewal.

We give thanks for the vision leading us to explore new District structures and pray that this will lead to more effective ways of working.

We give thanks for the continuing initiatives stimulated by Pray without Ceasing and pray that this will continue to encourage and challenge us in our life of prayer.

Ever-gracious God, forgive us when we fail you,
and encourage us when we seek you.
Ever-living God, forgive us when we go our own way,
and lead us to explore new life in you.
Ever-loving God, forgive us when we do not love,
and help us to know the reality of your love
revealed to us in Jesus.
So may we see you and know you, live in you and you in us,
know your love and respond with love for you and one another. Amen.

Diane Daymond, Deputy Chair, Plymouth and Exeter District

So often in my folly I live in poverty!
Not without money or possessions,
but self-denying the wealth of your love.
Living only to myself and not open to you.
Sometimes everything is different!
I realise that the gnawing hunger in my soul
can only be answered by denying self,
offering to you my weakness,
receiving again your cleansing forgiveness,
knowing that in you is a life of unlimited richness
    and fulfilment!
Glorious Lord and Saviour, I praise you! Amen.

Peter Fox, Local Preacher, Tavistock

Jesus
is Lord!
Creation's
voice
proclaims it.

H&P 260

65

Day 25

Praying with Christians in the Pacific

Jesus, abject and despised, let us not be ashamed to follow you. Jesus, hated and persecuted, let us not be afraid to walk in your footsteps. Jesus, blasphemed and condemned, let us be counted your friends. Jesus, mocked and scourged, let us bear all things patiently. Jesus, crowned and derided, let us not be overwhelmed by our injuries and grief. Amen.

John Wesley, 1703-91

Tonga

Methodist President:
'Alifalete Mone

Mission Partner:
ed Ruth Watt
th Marlene Wilkinson°

Scholarship Student:
Louisiale Uasike (Tonga)

Samoa

Methodist President:
Siatua Leulua 'iali'i

Scholarship Student:
Mosese Mailo-Fuaiva'a

Fiji

Methodist President:
Laisiasa Ratabacaca

Scholarship Students:
Timoci Nawaciono°
Josefa Turagacati° (in Fiji)

God of all, of fragile island and mighty continent,
we know you in the faithfulness of the tides,
we know you in the gentle sway of the palms,
we know you in the mighty strength of the cyclone,
and we worship you.
Jesus Christ, Saviour of all,
we know you in the traditions of faith,
we know you in the song and dance offered to your glory,
we know you in our lives through the love of those around us,
and we worship you.
Holy Spirit, alive in all your people,
we know you in the faithfulness of your Church,
we know you in the challenge to reach out in mission,
we know you in the lives of those who reach out to us,
and we worship you.
God of all, Saviour Christ, living Spirit,
we worship you in the Church,
we worship you in the world,
we worship you in our lives. Amen.

*Adrian Burdon, former Mission Partner, **Tonga***

Here is a sacred place. We are here because God is present. We are here to bear testimony to the sacredness of God. But more than anything else, we are here because God has called us to stand in solidarity with those who suffer unjustly. Lord Jesus, you are love and you see all the suffering and injustices in the world. Have pity, we pray, especially on those who are suppressed, unheard, marginalized and downtrodden because of culture and systems of government or by selfish friends and neighbours. We pray for women and children who suffer because of violence: at home, through political instability and ethnic tension. Look mercifully on them and those who are sorrowing. May Christians speak boldly on their behalf so that your kingdom, justice and mercy will reign in the world. Amen.

*Muriel Rogers**

*Previously published in a workshop manual by SPATS (South Pacific Association of Theological schools), Suva, Fiji. Used with permission.

Give thanks for the slowly-improving community relations in many divided parts of the District and for those working to build trust in the community.

Pray for many migrant workers coming into the area; that churches will welcome the alien and stranger as they should;

for the many ministers who have heavy workloads;

for ministers who have suffered ill-health in recent years.

Portadown District

Chair:
David Clements

We give thanks for the District Good News Roadshows which enable people to explore resources for mission;

for the commitment and energy of circuits across the District as they review their life and explore new ways of working and being the Church.

We pray for Churches in both urban and rural situations who are seeking to respond to those in their communities who are experiencing high levels of deprivation and stress;

for the work of the Synod Secretary, the Revd John Simms.

Sheffield District

Chair:
Vernon Marsh

Mission Partners:
Jonathan° and Elizabeth Gichaara, Neene, Israel and Muthomi (Kenya)

© Sheffield District

Generous God,
we thank you that, time after time,
in the most surprising places,
you spread a table for us
and welcome us to the feast
of your presence.
Sometimes we feel like amazed guests
at a banquet, a great celebration;
sometimes we meet you at a kitchen table
among friends, sharing daily bread;
sometimes as children enjoying a picnic,
laughing, singing, in the sunshine;
sometimes in a dark valley, on a hard journey,
by the barbed wire, bread is broken.
Always we find nourishment,
always enough for all who come:
we see that no one is ever turned away
and always we are blessed by sharing –
this is the gospel feast.
Thank you for such good food,
giving strength to do your work in the world,
and for your welcome at our journey's end. Amen.

Jan Sutch Pickard, lay preacher, Mull

We bring our varying gifts to thee, and thou rejectest none.

H&P 717

67

Day 26

Praying with Christians in Europe

Forgive us, O Lord, when we listen, but do not hear; when we look, but do not see; and when we feel, but do not act; and by your mercy and grace draw us into the righteous deeds of your kingdom of justice and peace; through Christ our Lord. Amen.

Maria Hare, 1798-1870

The United Methodist Northern Europe Central Conference

Bishop: Öystein Olsen

Superintendents:
Norway: Vidar Sten Bjerkseth, Øyvind Helliesen

Sweden: Bimbi Ollberg, Åke Svensson

Denmark: Ole Birch, Jørgen Thaarup

Finland (Swedish language) Tom Hellsten, Fredrik Wegelius

Finland (Finnish language) Timo Virtanen

Estonia: Taavi Hollman
Scholarship Student: Maire Ivanova°

Latvia: Gita Mednis
Scholarship Student: Inese Budnika° (in Britain)

Lithuania: John Campbell

Russia: Bishop of the UMC in Eurasia: Hans Vaxby
Mission Partner: p Nicola Vidamour°

Father God, we give you thanks for the life and work of the Methodist Church in **Estonia** in its centenary year. We thank you that, despite the repression and martyrdom of the Soviet era, there are now 26 congregations and new churches that have been built, including the Agape Centre in Pärnu and the theological seminary in Tallinn.
We pray for the Superintendent, Taavi Hollman; for those training for ministry at the Baltic Mission Centre; for the work of the Agape Centre, and for the pastor, Tonu Kuusemaa, youth minister, Maire Ivanova, and the team who run the church and school, as they serve you in a new world.

Tony Buglass, Superintendent Minister, Upper Calder Circuit

We pray for our brothers and sisters in **Latvia** as they strive to rebuild their churches and country. You have given them an opportunity to live and worship in freedom again. Give them your wisdom, your guidance, your strength and your perseverance. Fuel the spark that gave them hope during the many years of darkness so that they may be your welcoming light to all. We pray for the pastors and leaders of the church, its Sunday School teachers, and its members young and old. Amen.

Gita Mednis, Minister of 1st United Methodist Church, Riga, Latvia

Holy God, we rejoice that nothing in all creation can separate us from your love:
    neither the height of our tall apartment blocks
    nor the breadth of our vast country,
    nor the length of our cold, dark winters.
You keep us in your grasp as firmly as the ice holds the frozen river.
You wrap us in your warm embrace as tightly as our winter coats and scarves.
You stretch out your hand to support us whenever we feel we are going to slip or fall.
May we see your grace in every snowflake and walk in your footprints each day of our lives. Amen.

Snowy Pskov, Russia, Nicola Vidamour

*Nicola Vidamour, Mission Partner, Pskov, **Russia***

Southampton District

Chair:
Andrew Wood

Give thanks for the commitment to fresh expressions of being church which have taken hold in the life of our District over the last 12 months;
for the gracious tension between old and new;
for courage to take risks in the name of the kingdom.
We pray for places where the Church is working alongside those in need;
for the growing number of children's, youth and family workers employed by the circuits,
for partnerships with local authorities and agencies;
that those taking imaginative steps of faith will be nurtured and supported;
for all those we meet on the journey.

Loving God,
where can we find you, but in the lives of those in need?
Where can we join you, except in the taking of risks for the sake of the kingdom?
And yet, God of grace, you find us, you join us.
In our living and in our praying, you are there.
May we keep alert to the possibilities brought to us by your Son, Jesus, and ride the wave of your Spirit. Amen.

Andrew Wood, Southampton District Chair

Now is the time to
speak your mind,
to make yourself heard;
to make a noise
for
holy justice.
for all things are ready.

Now is the time to
let the cries of the world
be heard;
the groans of creation,
the pains of separation,
for all things are ready now.

Hear our prayers, O Lord, and let
our cries come to you. Amen.

*Margaret Sawyer, Connexional
Women's Network Secretary*

With power, with justice, he will walk his way.

H&P 140

Day 27

Praying with Christians in Europe

Look, O Christ, upon our sin-stained consciences and cleanse them with your precious blood. Look upon our divided hearts and heal them by your redeeming grace. Look upon our languid spirits, kindle in them the fire of your perfect love; through Christ our Lord. Amen.

William Booth, 1829-1912

Belgium
President of the Église Protestante Unie:
Daniel Vanescote

The United Methodist Central Conference of Germany
Bishop:
Rosemarie Wenner

Mission Partners:
p Colin° and Muriel Barrett
p Barry° and Gillian Sloan, Michael and Megan

We give thanks for good experiences in church planting and renewal of established congregations in the three Annual Conferences (North, East, South) in **Germany**;
for new members from all over the world who have been received into German congregations and for the increasing ministry with migrants throughout the country.
We pray for God's guidance as new congregations are built up; for example, a congregation for young people aged 15-30 in Karlsruhe.

We pray that God will open our eyes, our hearts and our minds so that we as Methodists, together with our partner churches, will share the gospel and will respond to the needs of our neighbours in our secularized society.

Bishop Rosemarie Wenner,
United Methodist Central Conference of Germany

Faith, hope, love
Heavenly Father,
I am of such little faith,
I see your ways,
but I do not walk them.
I understand your love,
but I do not love the same.
Help me to keep faith with you.
Where the best is the enemy of the good,
help me to know your good.
Where an absence of conflict is the enemy of peace,
help me to pursue your peace.
And through all the issues of this day,
be my guide. Amen.

James Church, URC Ordinand, Cambridge

Give thanks to God for the strong sense of connectedness we feel across the hills, valleys and urban centres of our District enabling us to help one another respond better to the call of Christ today.

We pray for those who are confused and uncertain about changing traditional and well-loved 'chapel culture' in order to reach out to those who do not know the stories of Jesus; for our Mission Enabling Team who are leading the District's response to 'Our Calling', creating our 'Priorities' and offering in this place all things in Christ.

West Yorkshire District

Chair:
Peter Whittaker

> May the compelling love of Christ for life on the earth drive us, as disciples, to hallow
> the air we breathe
> the water we drink
> the food we eat
> the company we keep
> the communities we create
> so that love may permeate whole lives,
> all life, and the planet itself. Amen.
>
> *Peter Whittaker, West Yorkshire District Chair*

Garsdale Scar (© Diane Coleman)

Lord, in the quietness of the early morning
with the new day before me,
give me the strength and encouragement
to meet the challenges that this new day brings.

(Silent reflection)

Lord, in the middle of the day,
in the midst of the daily round,
I hear stories and see pictures that remind me of a world
where life for many people is so different from mine.
Help me, through the power of your Holy Spirit
to put my priorities into place.

(Silent reflection)

Lord, at the end of the day,
when I leave the thoughts of this busy day behind,
come to my weary soul,
with your caring love that offers rest in you. Amen.

Pam Turner, Connexional Women's Network President 2007-8

He is love,
he is love.

H&P 565

Day 28

Praying with Christians in Central Europe

Jesus, by your wounded feet, direct our path aright. Jesus, by your nailed hands, move us to deeds of love. Jesus, by your pierced side, cleanse our desires. Jesus, by your broken heart, knit ours to yours. Amen.

Richard Crawshaw, 1613-49

United Methodist Central and Southern Europe Central Conference

Bishop:
Bishop Dr Patrick Streiff

Superintendents:
Algeria:
Daniel Nussbaumer

Austria: Lothar Poell

Bulgaria:
Bedros Altunian

Czech Republic:
Josef Cervenak

Georgia

Slovak Republic:
Robert Zachar

Hungary: Istvan Csernak

Poland: Edward Puslecki, Jan Ostry, Zbigniew Kaminski
Scholarship Student:
Janusz Daszuta°
(in Poland)
France: Daniel Nussbaumer

Switzerland: Markus Bach, Elsi Atorfer, Martin Streit

We pray for **Bulgaria** in its first years of its membership of the European Union;
for those who are excited by it and those who are afraid of it;
for the leaders of the country;
for people with difficult jobs and long working hours and those without work;
for the hungry, the vulnerable and those living in the many institutions (orphanages, psychiatric hospitals and homes for the elderly).
We pray for the Methodist Church, in the difficulties it faces and for its pastors, and we give thanks for its members who, through a difficult past, have kept a strong faith.

Pete and Samantha Taylor, former Mission Partners in Bulgaria

Almighty Father, we glorify your name for all you have done for **Slovakia**. The Methodist Church there is very small but we believe that you have great things planned. Let its members be a tool in your hands to bring the Gospel to the Slovakian people. There are still many who do not know of the amazing love and forgiveness you have for them. Lead them and make them faithful to their task of proclaiming your name. Amen.

Lenka Prochazkova, Missions Co-ordinator, UMC Slovakia

O God, Spirit within us, you hold everyone in your embrace. You give us a vision of a new world of love
and peace and justice,
where resources are shared fairly within
the global family,
where different races live in harmony and nations seek the way of peace,
where everyone is able to live a full, abundant life.
Help us to have a genuine concern for our neighbour remembering that everyone is your concern, and that in serving others we are serving you. Amen.

Superintendent Minister, Hinchley Circuit, Northampton District

We give thanks for the success of the recent Environmental Conference at Church Stretton entitled 'Think of a World . . .' and for continuing work with the Marches Energy Agency as the District seeks to increase awareness of how to be better stewards of creation;

for those ministers and congregations who are encouraging new ways of being Christ's disciples in the world;

for unsung heroes in churches large or small across the District who demonstrate love in action every day.

We pray for the Lay Stationing Representative, David Kirby, the District Mission Enabler, Revd Andrew Roberts and the Training and Development Officer, Charles Worth;

for the newly launched District 'Komera' Project which focuses on Rwanda and aims to support the hospital in Kibogora, as well as the work of Pharp – which seeks to bring health, peace and reconciliation to those scarred by conflict in that country.

Wolverhampton and Shrewsbury District

Chair:
John Howard

Mission Partners:
Daniel° and Laura Williams, Danny, Debbie and Damaris (Cuba)

Lord Jesus Christ, who fled as a refugee to Egypt, lived as a carpenter's son in Nazareth, whose father died while he was young, who travelled the streets of Palestine and walked the long road to the cross, help us in a time of change when we fear losing even the things we thought would be with us all our lives. Help us to learn how to trust in you, who is the same yesterday, today and for ever, and in that security to embrace the future with joy and obedience. Amen.

John Howard, Wolverhampton and Shrewsbury District Chair

All-seeing, all-embracing, all-loving God,
Creator and re-creator of us all,
whose word is his deed,
who stretches out a hand to steady those who stumble,
who lifts the fallen,
and binds up the wounds of those most damaged
in the struggles of life,
fill your people with the desire to become more like you,
so that,
when we hear the cries of those in need,
when we listen to the groaning of our fragile world,
when we meet the stranger and fear to call them 'friend',
we too may see all, embrace all, and love all
in deed as well as word.
In Christ's name we pray. Amen.

Sue Huband, Wem and Prees Green Circuit

Make me a captive Lord, and then I shall be free.

H&P 714

73

Day 29

Praying with Christians in Central Europe

Be to us, O Lord Jesus Christ, the table set for all, the inextinguishable light of the saints, the sun shining in our midst and the joy and grace of your people; now and for ever. Amen.

Symeon the New Theologian, 949-1022

United Methodist Central and Southern Europe Central Conference (continued)

Serbia and
   Montenegro:
Superintendent:
Ana Palik-Kuncak

Macedonia:
Superintendent:
Wilhelm Nausner

We thank God for people working for peace and reconciliation in the Balkans. We give you thanks for the Centre for Non-violence, Peace and Reconciliation in Osijek, Croatia. We praise you for relationships stretching across the boundaries of culture, ethnicity, language and faith which give witness to your loving intention that people should be members of one human family, and which challenge nationalistic values of domination and fear.

We pray for the future peace of **Kosovo**, **Bosnia-Herzegovena**, **Macedonia**, **Serbia**, **Montenegro** and **Croatia**. We hold before you all who work for better relationships and understanding between the different peoples who live there. We pray for people searching for loved ones killed and still missing in the Balkan conflicts of the 1990s; for divided communities torn apart through ethnic cleansing; for war veterans who feel betrayed and abandoned by their own governments. We pray for a healing of memories and a renewal of hope in places of despair. We pray for justice among the nations, reconciliation among the peoples and a building of a genuine and lasting peace in this part of Europe.

Colin Ride, World Church Secretary, Europe

We pray for the Church in Serbia, for God's helping hand as they negotiate the return of Church property which was nationalized after World War II. We pray for hope and strength during this lengthy journey, and for his wisdom in exploring the future purpose of these properties that the doors might open on new ministries. We pray for a renewal of the whole Church in Serbia, in Christ's name. Amen.

Superintendent Ana Palik-Kuncak, Kisac/Serbia

As St Paul long ago answered the call to come and help in Macedonia, may Christians in Macedonia also respond to your call to help others, especially those without jobs, children living in severe poverty and elderly people with no one to care for them. In Christ's name. Amen.

Carol Partridge, Missionary in Strumica/Macedonia

As another month draws to an end we give thanks for the days that have passed and for any opportunities for service we have grasped. In penitence for times when we have failed to live up to our calling, we confidently accept your forgiving love. Remembering especially the recent commemoration of the role played by William Wilberforce in the abolition of the slave trade and his roots in Hull, we acknowledge with pain that people still live in bondage, and we commit ourselves to continue to strive to set all free. Loving and gracious God, you have been with us in the days that are now past, you walk with us today and you will remain with us in all that is to come. For your unfailing steadfast love we offer our thanks. Amen.

We pray for inner-city and for rural communities, that there may be a developing understanding of the challenges and opportunities each other face;
for new initiatives in Hull, with increasing co-operation between circuits and with the North Humberside Industrial Mission;
for ongoing ecumenical dialogue, especially with the Diocese of York and the United Reformed Church;
for the District's new Synod Secretary, Heather Shipman, as she begins her term of office.

York and Hull District

Chair:
Stephen Burgess

Mission Partners:
David° and Jessie Wee
  (Singapore)

'For inasmuch . . .'
Help me to meet you today, Lord,
in the one I share a joke with,
in the one who takes time to listen to my grumbles,
in the one I would rather avoid talking to,
in the one who needs a hand.
May I recognize you in all your children
and act accordingly.
In Jesus' name. Amen.

David Walton, Local Preacher, Eccles

A special prayer for 29 February
Providing God, for this extra day and all that it will contain, for the extra hours to spend as your disciples, for any chances to live life to the full, we thank you, and may we leap for joy as we reflect on your creation. Amen.

Stephen Burgess, York and Hull District Chair

What a blessing to know that Jesus is mine!
H&P 563

Day 30

Praying with Christians in Southern Europe

God the Father, eternally mysterious, we worship you. God the Son, eternally responding, we bless you. God the Holy Spirit, eternally witnessing, we adore you. Holy and glorious Trinity, three persons and one God, we magnify you, now and for ever. Amen.

Nestorian Liturgy, 5th century

Portugal
Bishop:
Sifredo Teixeira
rt Cora Aspey

Spain Iglesia Evangelica Española
President:
Joel Cortès

Italy
Methodist President:
Massimo Aquilante

Mission Partners:
p Augusto° and Mirna Giron, Gabriel and Debora

Dear God, we thank you very much for all that you have been doing for and through the Portuguese Methodist Church. Accept our gratitude for all those that you have been using to help the Church.

Through the joys and the difficulties they face may they find you and feel closer to you. There are many needs in **Portugal**, but we ask you to guide the Church in its priority mission of sharing the good news with many people who are without hope, love, joy and acceptance. We praise your name. We give you our love. May you continue to bless all of your Church in Portugal. We pray in Jesus' name. Amen.

Sifredo Teixeira, Bishop of Portugal

We pray for the staff and students of the United Evangelical Seminary (SEUT) in El Escorial, **Spain**. Strengthen and guide them as they prepare local church leaders in the Spanish-speaking world. We also pray for the Church in Spain as it strives to assimilate newly arrived immigrants. Some people in Spain feel the country is being flooded with immigrants. This is very difficult for a country that was isolated for so long. Although it can be experienced as a challenge, open their eyes to see it as a gift of divine grace. Many who come already know you, and they will be the instruments of bringing Christ to many Spaniards. All over the world, you come to us in fresh ways in our immigrant sisters and brothers and enrich our faith. Open our hearts to receive your grace, as we give ourselves to serve in the name of Jesus, the one who left all to serve us. Amen.

Marcos Abbott, Dean, United Evangelical Seminary

We pray that in Christ Italians might find the purpose of life;
that in Christ Italians may receive the love of God;
that in Christ Italians may receive the peace of God;
that in Christ Italians may obtain the joy of God.

Augusto Giron, Mission Partner, Italy

Scotland District

Chair:
Lily Twist

We give thanks for the work of Action of Churches Together in Scotland (ACTS), its core staff; for the programme and hospitality of Scottish Churches House;
for circuits engaged in mission-led re-formation.
We pray for the Revd Lily Twist, the new District Chair;
for the contemporary mission of the Church in Scotland.

All-encompassing God, you challenge us in so many ways.
May we hear your voice when you call and obey your word.
Give us patience to know that you hear our prayer
and will answer when the time is right. Amen.

Helen Anderson, Paisley

Amid the uncertainties of continual change, Spirit of God, guide us as we face the challenges of being your people, the Church, today. Help us as we pray to accept your call. Grant us courage to step out in faith with the message of Christ, that God's love and forgiveness may be known by all. Amen.

Angela Dobbins

*Cloisters at Iona Abbey
(© Diane Coleman)*

Shetland District

Chair:
Jeremy Dare

We thank you, God, for the children and young people who are part of the life of the Shetland District.
We pray for them and those who minister to them in Christian activities;
for those involved with our churches who are giving much for the work of the kingdom of God in this District, especially the pastoral visitors, local preachers and musicians;
for the work of the Synod Secretary, Sylvia White, and the Senior Circuit Steward, Peter Tait;
for wisdom for those who seek to help people in the community for whom alcohol and drugs are so important.

Almighty God, we want to bless you with our praise this day.
For the amazing variety of colour and texture,
movement and life in creation,
    we thank you.
For the wonder of your love reaching out to us in Jesus
with saving grace and the gift of eternal life,
    we worship you.
For the fruit and gifts of your Holy Spirit,
helping us to enjoy our faith, refresh our lives
and display your love in our communities,
    we offer you our praise. Amen.

Jeremy Dare, Shetland District Chair

How sweet the name of Jesus sounds.

H&P 257

Last day of the month

Praying with the World Council of Churches

Grant us your help, O God, that whatever by the teaching of your Holy Spirit we know to be our duty, we may by your grace be enabled to perform it; through Jesus Christ our Lord. Amen.

William Bright, 1824-1901

Mission Partners and others recently returned from overseas:

Michelle Adams (China)
Michael and Svetlana Armstrong (Japan)
Ian and Diana Bosman (Ghana)
Gareth Braisdell (Belize)
Jenny Butcher (Kenya)
Michael and Marion Dobson (India)
Marion Evans (Ghana)
Hannah Facey (Ghana)
Emily John (Ghana)
Elaine and Ewart Joseph (MCCA)
David Keenan (Nigeria)
Kate Keir (China)
Ros Leigh (India)
Andrew McLeod (China)
Andy and Sheila Moffoot (Kenya)
Claire Price (Zambia)
Margaret Scarlett (China)
Peter and Samantha Taylor (Bulgaria)
David Upp (Fiji)
Elaine and John Woolley (The Gambia)

Lord God, King of the universe, forgive us that we so easily forget that you are the creator of every human person whether they share our faith or not.
We place in your hands:
>   those who sense divinity in many and various ways
>   through the harmony of nature and the goodness
>   of humankind;
>   those you have called into covenant with you since
>   Abraham and who received your Torah
>   through Moses;
>   those who have responded to the Word in the Qur'an
>   and submit to the One God;
>   those who cannot believe and reject all revelation,
>   but seek justice and peace, beauty and truth.

May we learn from others, who belong to you whether they know it or not, to respect and enjoy the rich diversity of all that you have made, while celebrating the grace you have particularly granted to us in our Lord Jesus Christ. Amen.

Frances Young

Gracious God, I thank you and praise you
that the 'voice of prayer is never silent';
that the living Body of Christ stirs throughout the world, offering worship and prayer;
that the light of Christ is embedded in the hearts of
>   countless people, all known to you,

offering your love to their neighbours, both near and far;
that your loving care encircles me,
through all the experiences of life;
that I am part of the vast communion of saints,
>   unknown and unknowable, but united in you, God,
>   who is Parent, Son and Spirit;

that your kingdom is here on earth and will be completed in glory. Amen.

Frances Hopwood, Secretary, World Mission Forum

Gracious Creator God, we thank you for the blessing of your Church's colourful, loving expression around the world. We thank you for brothers and sisters we may never meet but who are intertwined with us through the kinship of Christ's fellowship. Empower us with clear thinking and great courage so that, wherever we live and in whatever capacity we can, we might lovingly speak truth to power and help to change oppressive systems that deprive human beings of their dignity. We ask this in the name of Jesus, our Teacher and Saviour. Amen.

Lisa Marchal, Elder, The United Methodist Church

Mission Partners in transit or training:
David Furnival
Leslie and Alison Judd

On being a mission partner
Show us all, Lord,
where we should be,
what we should give
and how to bring your love to all
so that our gifts may be used to honour you. Amen.

Samantha Taylor, former Mission Partner in Bulgaria

Tongan dancers
(Adrian Burdon)

REJOICE as a Cherokee Indian cradles her grandchild for the first time and in that precious, holy moment sees, reflected in this child, her own eternity.
REJOICE as a young African refugee creeps into an unfamiliar town centre church at midnight and, in the silence of candlelight, finds peace in the sanctuary for his troubled soul.
REJOICE as a Russian woman boldly proclaims to her atheist family: 'I have become a Christian.'
REJOICE at God's worldwide, timeless grace wrapping each of us in faith, hope and love. Amen.

Mollie Priest

A crowded church in China
(Ian Groves)

O God, Saviour of the world, you hold all humanity together.
You give us a worldwide family of sisters and brothers in Christ
with a rich diversity of culture and language and creed:
with gifts of hand and mind and heart.
with the experience of age, the challenge of youth,
the curiosity of children.
Help us to show respect and to value one another,
remembering that we are all made in your image. Amen.

Barbara Bircumshaw, Superintendent Minister,
Hinchley Circuit, Northampton District

He plants
his footsteps
in the sea and
rides upon
the storm.

H&P 65

79

Additional Resources

The Methodist website www.methodistchurch.org.uk
– includes notes on the daily readings and prayers from the
Prayer Handbook and other sources.

Magnet – the magazine of the Women's Network –
available from your local church or circuit distributor.
Details of individual subscriptions from the Women's
Network Office, Methodist Church House (MCH),
25 Marylebone Road, London NW1 5JR. Tel: 020 7486 5502.

Mission Matters – part of the Link Mailing – available from mph.

Words for Today (IBRA) – reflections on daily Bible readings
from many parts of the world and well-known writers.
Light for our Path (IBRA) – notes for those who need a
simpler and less provocative approach. Both are available
from mph.

The Methodist Recorder – from your newsagent or
122 Golden Lane, London EC1Y 0TL.

The Prayer Handbook on Tape – from Galloways Society for
the Blind, Howick House, Howick Park Avenue, Penwortham,
Preston PR1 0LS. Tel: 01772 753705.

Prayer Focus – The Prayer Handbook of the Methodist Church
in Ireland – available from the Methodist Church in Ireland,
No 9 Resources Centre, 9 Lennoxvale, Belfast BT9 5BY.

*We are always looking for new writers so, if you feel
inspired to write something for the 2008-9 handbook, please
send your contribution by the end of February 2008 to
editorial@quantrillmedia.com or Primavera Quantrill, Editor,
Methodist Prayer Handbook, mph, 4 John Wesley Road,
Peterborough PE4 6ZP.*

Copyright – prayers in this book are © 2007 Trustees for Methodist
Church Purposes, unless otherwise indicated. Churches are
free to use them in public worship and reproduce up to 10
prayers in magazines or newsletters during the year providing
acknowledgement is given.

Printed by **Swan Print and Design**, Shuttleworth Road, Elms Farm
Industrial Estate, Bedford MK41 0EP.

Key – The letters beside
the names indicate the
type of work in which
Mission Partners are
mainly engaged:

ad administration
ag agriculture
d doctor
ed education
m medical work (other
than doctor or nurse)
n nurse
p pastoral worker
rt retired
sd social/development
work
sp special partner
t technical
th theological training
° minister
* deacon

+ Joint Appointment
USPG United Society for
the Propagation of the
Gospel (Anglican)
CMS Church Mission
Society (Anglican)
CofS Church of Scotland
CA Christians Abroad
NMA Nationals in
Mission Appointments
UCA United College of
the Ascension
WCBP World Church in
Britain Partnership
CWM Council for World
Mission

Tongan Dancers (Adrian Burdon)